THE EVOLUTION OF SKATING

SK8RZ PASSION, OUR STORY

VOLUME III

Amirah Palmer

Printed in the United States of America

Published by
SK8RZ Konnect
5340 Weslayan St., Unit #273323
Houston, Texas 77005
eMail: publisher@sk8rzkonnect.com
Website: www.sk8rzkonnect.com

ISBN: 979-8-9865272-9-1

Library of Congress Control Number: 2022912127

Book Cover and Interior Design:
Jessica Tilles of TWASolutions.com

Special discounts are available on quantity purchases by corporations, associations, educators, and others. For details, contact the publisher.

All SK8RZ Konnect titles are distributed by:
Ingram Content
www.ingramcontent.com

Dedications

After giving honor to Allah (swt) and with heartfelt love and gratitude, I dedicate this book to:

To all those who have believed in, supported, contributed to, and assisted me in creating and sharing this book series, I extend my deepest gratitude. What started as a dream has evolved into a vision, culminating in the manifestation of a book series. Our collective drive has always been to leave a lasting legacy, our legacy, documenting the essence of the skate community and culture in our own words, for the world to see.

I express heartfelt thanks to everyone who has participated in this endeavor, both present contributors and those with future plans to join in shaping this legacy by sharing their journey.

Acknowledgments

"Unity is strength...when there is teamwork and collaboration, wonderful things can be achieved."

–Mattie Stepanek

Roller skating transcends being merely a sport; it evolves into an art, a manifestation of personal expression on wheels. Each skater silently communicates the thoughts of their mind, the emotions of their heart, and the unique experiences they wish to share. It's not a skill learned; it's a sensation felt. While there exists a framework of style and rhythm, the individual's expression is distinctly their own.

No two skaters will provide an identical experience. Despite similar moves, the feelings inspiring those actions stem from their unique life journeys. This acknowledgment extends to a remarkable tribe of talented, skilled, educated, and dedicated individuals contributing to this project, both directly and indirectly. In the introspection of 2022, I realized that this book was my dream, and none of you initially signed up for this venture. Yet, collaboratively, we are crafting history, leaving behind a legacy to cherish, all to preserve and safeguard a beloved culture.

Special thanks to those who visually catalog our artistry: Linwood Neverson of Sk8Kingz Media, Doug Mike of Sk8 Vidzz, Terrance Glover of Triple 7 Magazine, Sk8CultureClub, Wes Jiggs, Jayson Vernon, Chad Harrell of SkateLyfe TV, Robert Dea, David Pippen of SkatePhotos.com, Roll Modul, Tyrone Dennis, Malik Thomas of Sk8 Chicago, Scotty Moson, Dr. L. David Stewart of Year60 Photography, Rogelio Valdez, Kurby Brown, Fabrice Bueno, Chuck Williams of

WBSA TV, Debra Chase of Timeless Connections, KappaChris Robinson, Short Shots, Larry Black, Timeless Connections, Glennesha Johnson of DWL Studios, Scott Rinaldi of Scott Rinaldi Photography, Above Ground Photography, Sk8Luv33, Nate Wren, Queen City Skate TV, Ron Fussnecker of Midwest Skaters and the many others who have contributed and are nameless, I thank you and send a wealth of gratitude to you all. Forgive me for those not mentioned. Charge it to my mind and not my heart.

Peace and Blessings to all,

Amirah Palmer

Contents

Preface

"Out of every adversity, comes opportunity."

– Benjamin Franklin

This quote resonates deeply, particularly in the context of the COVID-19 pandemic that forced a significant shift in our daily, work, and social lives. The virus's impact has been profound, rearranging life in unexpected ways. Whether through personal experiences with friends, family, or coworkers, we have all been touched by the pandemic's effects—ranging from early deaths, unemployment, to loneliness and financial instability.

The pandemic prompted a forced stillness, compelling individuals to sit, focus, and recalibrate their lives. It was a moment where the realization of not being in control became apparent. In the silence, people began to grow, reevaluate life from a different perspective, and face the choice of sinking or swimming. Financial struggles were intensified for those already on the brink, and health battles were waged with some facing lingering issues.

The same held true for me. During the pandemic, I hosted a podcast where skaters would visit my studio to share their experiences, history, and passion for roller skating. When quarantined, I had to shift and began conducting interviews via Zoom. As I adapted, a concern crept into my soul—what if this history, our history, is lost? How can I ensure our stories are preserved? Books have always stood the test of time, so I thought of writing a book, a logical choice. But where do I begin? Seeking guidance, I called Ice From Philly, seeking his advice and blessings on this journey. After thorough discussions, he saw the merit in this endeavor and agreed to assist, connecting me with individuals who could contribute to this meaningful project. To him, I am forever grateful.

I aim to take you on a journey into the heart of skate culture, unraveling the passion that fuels our love for the art and sport. This collaborative effort brings together members of the skate community, sharing their stories of introduction, acceptance, growth, and mastery in the artistry and skill of roller skating. I welcome you to immerse yourself in the passion of each contributor, gaining insight into the unique roles we all play in shaping this culture. The evolution of roller skating continues to unfold, offering a versatile experience that can be enjoyed alone or with family and friends. It stands as an inclusive activity, welcoming individuals regardless of race, religion, social, or financial status.

As you delve into each narrative, I encourage you to approach it with an open heart, engage your mind, connect with your soul, and embrace the unfolding journey—the crafty and innovative.

Peace and Blessings

Amirah Palmer

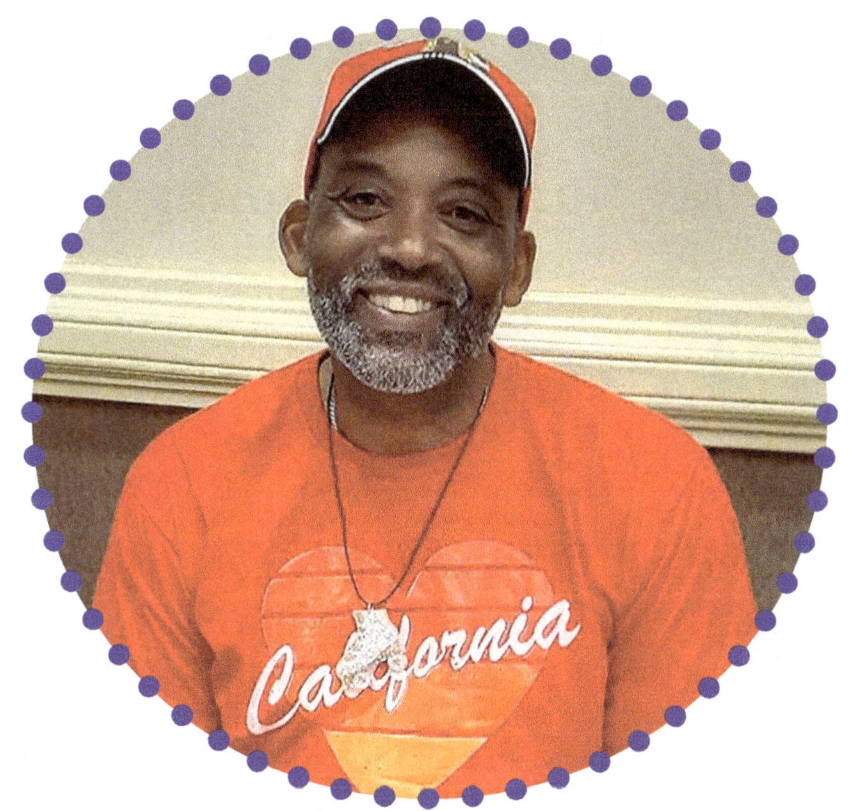

Richard Humphrey

aka RollerDanceMan

Facebook: @Richard Humphrey | Instagram: @RichardHumphrey

"My Humble Beginning"

My skate journey began as a young five-year-old in 1957, growing up in the Fillmore District of San Francisco where I was born and raised. Skating on metal skates with family and friends was the coolest thing to do. Bowling was my real passion in the early '60s. When the skate bug hit me again in the early '70s, about 1975, I hit the rink and never looked back. Grand Arena Roller Rink in Southern San Francisco was the place to be. Fast Forward to 1978, I did a Christmas Show wearing an all-white tuxedo with white patent leather shoes.

At that moment, I said to myself, "It would be so cool to have my own skate boot line!"

Yes, it was a big dream I hoped it would happen one day. In 1979, other skaters and I auditioned for a TV pilot called, *Dancing Wheels,* just before the movie, *Roller Boogie,* came out. It would have been one of the hottest shows on eight wheels, but it never made it.

In the early '80s, some really cool things did happen, we kept hearing about Venice Beach so I went to check it out to see their styles, which were very different from ours. I was always curious about other skate styles. If you've never gone to Venice Beach, you must put it on your list of places to skate.

In 1981, our group the Golden Rollers traveled to Los Angeles only to be challenged by a roller group called the Scooby Brothers, which was a great battle. We did not share our moves because we were

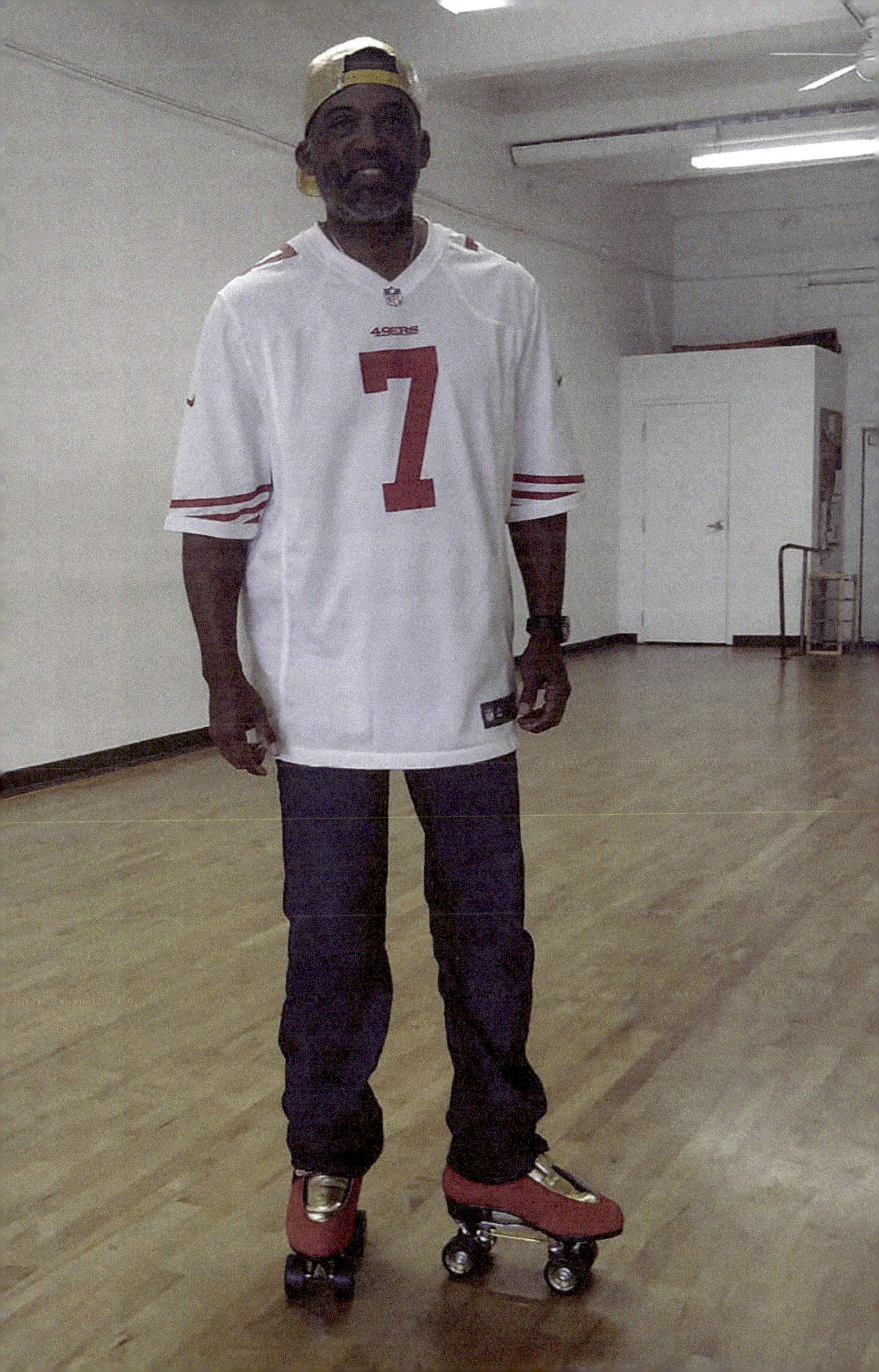
49ERS
7

performers and not wanting others to copy our moves. It wasn't till years later that I would share my steps with the world. Social Media also played a large role in this as well.

Another great event was that the Director of the San Francisco Ballet, Michael Smuin—discovered our group, The Golden Rollers in Golden Gate. Almost immediately, he wanted us to perform at one of his ballet concerts. It was a great experience. Little did I know that the CEO of my company was in attendance that night. That was awesome. The following year we did some cool things like appearing on a popular TV show in 1982 called, *Evening Magazine* followed up in 83' by Another big TV show called, *Real People*. In 1985 we did an opening for the comedian Phyllis Diller, in Oakland, CA—along with other cool guest spots. Fast-forwarding to after the group broke up, I continued my journey surrounded by great positive people.

The year 2006 was amazing. I went on to do a feature story in one of the biggest Black magazines in the world, Ebony Magazine. My great friend, DJ Spin from Los Angeles—was also chronicled in these esteemed pages. Talk about awesome! That same year, the owner of Skates on Haight, my friend, Lee Cole— had some ideas on a new skate setup. Lee called them Quadlines—a cross between Quad Skates and Inline Skates. He called me for my ideas, shortly after that we put out one of the first skate infomercials on the internet. It was a hit!

My Slogan was, "It's A Whole New Skating Experience."

During this time other opportunities came about. Comedian Damon Wayans was doing a sitcom called *Damon Wayans*: *The Underground* and needed a stunt double to do a skate scene. Well, I got the call from their team to fly out to Los Angeles to be that stunt double on TV! What an experience. The Quadline photo became heavily featured in Ebony and also Damon wanted a pair—which I built for him. Quadline became quite the hot seller. It also became my first endorsed product which sold thousands of units worldwide. I created a similar skate called The Streamline, which has 100mm wheels instead of a standard quad wheel.

My license plate today says, "Quadline." To top it off, the wheel was also my signature wheel—with my autograph imprinted on the trundle.

Remember—dreams do come true! Moving from 1978 to 2009, Lee Cole put a call into Riedell about my cool idea—and they liked it. It would be the first-ever Riedell Skate Boot with no laces. I coined the name, Richard Humphrey No Strings Attached. At that time, I only had one-hundred pairs made. Nevertheless, history was in the making by the first person of color to have their own boot line. This accomplishment followed up with Rollerbones Inc., the biggest name brand in roller skate wheels. I had them make The RH Silver Rollerbones followed by RH Golden Rollers Rollerbones named after The Golden Rollers. Very few roller skate companies have ever had wheels named after anyone. I will never forget this opportunity thanks to Lee Cole who is no longer with us—but his memory will live on. The year 2009 got better I got a call from The Dr. Oz show to come in and teach him some dance moves. How cool was that? The live studio audience taping aired in 2010. I always had a desire to be on the Oprah Show—and it happened. I was also voted into The Skaters Hall of Fame by my fellow skaters as a Lifetime Award. I am truly humbled!

So, when we talk about the inspiration that person can be anyone and, in my case, I watched Denise Austin a Fitness Guru on TV every morning and she had videos.

I said to myself, "What roller skaters have instructional video?"

No one did, so my video journey began. With all of my notes from the '70s to 80's I had enough material to create the *Roller Dancing: A Workout on Skates* instructional video. It shows thirteen of the hottest steps on skates in a dance form that no one ever experienced on skates. This is truly one of the best workouts on skates today. Currently, these very moves are now seen all over the entire skate world. Because of Denise Austin, I saw her series of videos that featured every exercise you can imagine. So, I followed my gut and continued to create some eleven instructional videos—for any level skater—from Backward Skating to advanced danced routines/choreography.

Today I teach many of those steps from the past - not from the 1900s as some have suggested. The '70s and '80s were the mecca of many dance moves you see today. With that being said, a lot of today's moves are from moves of the past– originating from so many of our greatest skaters. We are just passing it on to those that want to learn—and preserve the culture going into the future.

My motto is, "You control the roll, don't let the roll control you."

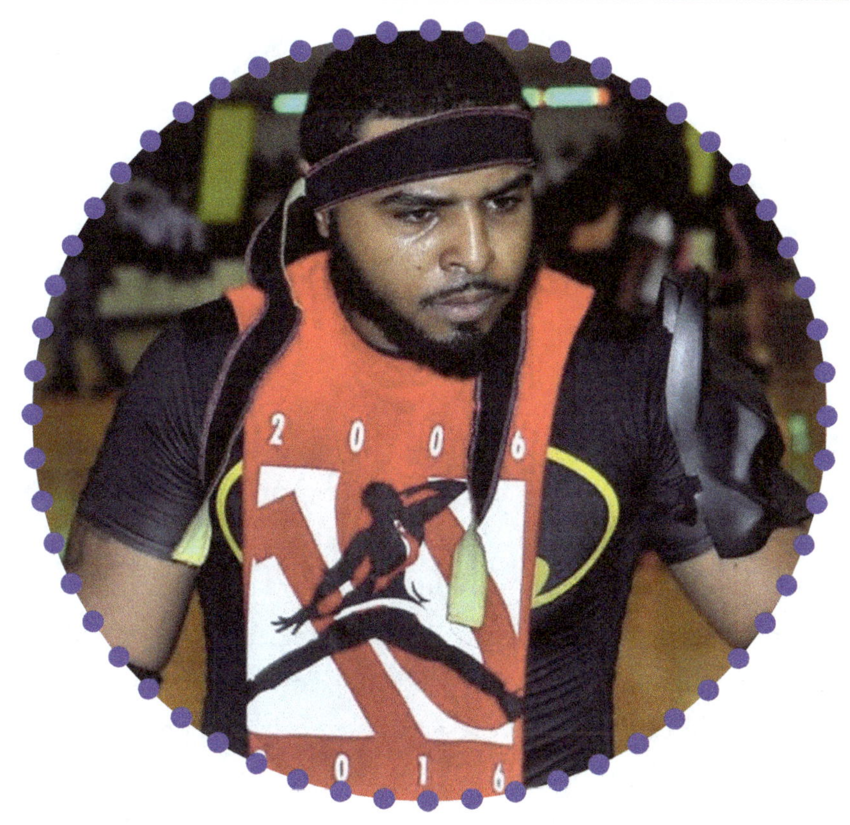

Joshua Smith

aka Batsmoke

Facebook: @Josh Smith | Instagram: @ josh_batsmoke

"Man vs. Mask—The Bat"

Riddle me this, riddle me that—are you sure you want to be in the mind of the BAT? Who, or what is this entity? The BAT is energy fueled by energy, passion for the art of roller skating. He is the epitome of elite entertainment. Changing the atmosphere is what he does. Helping those around him cut loose from the ties of code-switching everyday life presents us once they enter the skating arena. His creativity is beyond measure and pushing the boundaries of the rules is what he thrives on. No fear or intimidation of crowds or magnitude of task moves him. This man is clutch. He loves to inspire. Good Ol' Bat wears the mask only to mask the man behind it. Being in an environment that can be the ultimate source of validation can consume one. But the journey to find truth in self in a place of fantasy is a long road of life lessons. Platform after platform learning that he is more than I want him to be in my previous selfish heart. To finally see that representation of self reflects a world that watches. I now know what he means and what his purpose truly is.

No legacy stands only by what one does—but by the impact of what he does on those that matter. Love is the answer.

Knowing my place—I'm here to bring joy and happiness. I'm here to teach and encourage. I'm here to create and inspire. I'm here to

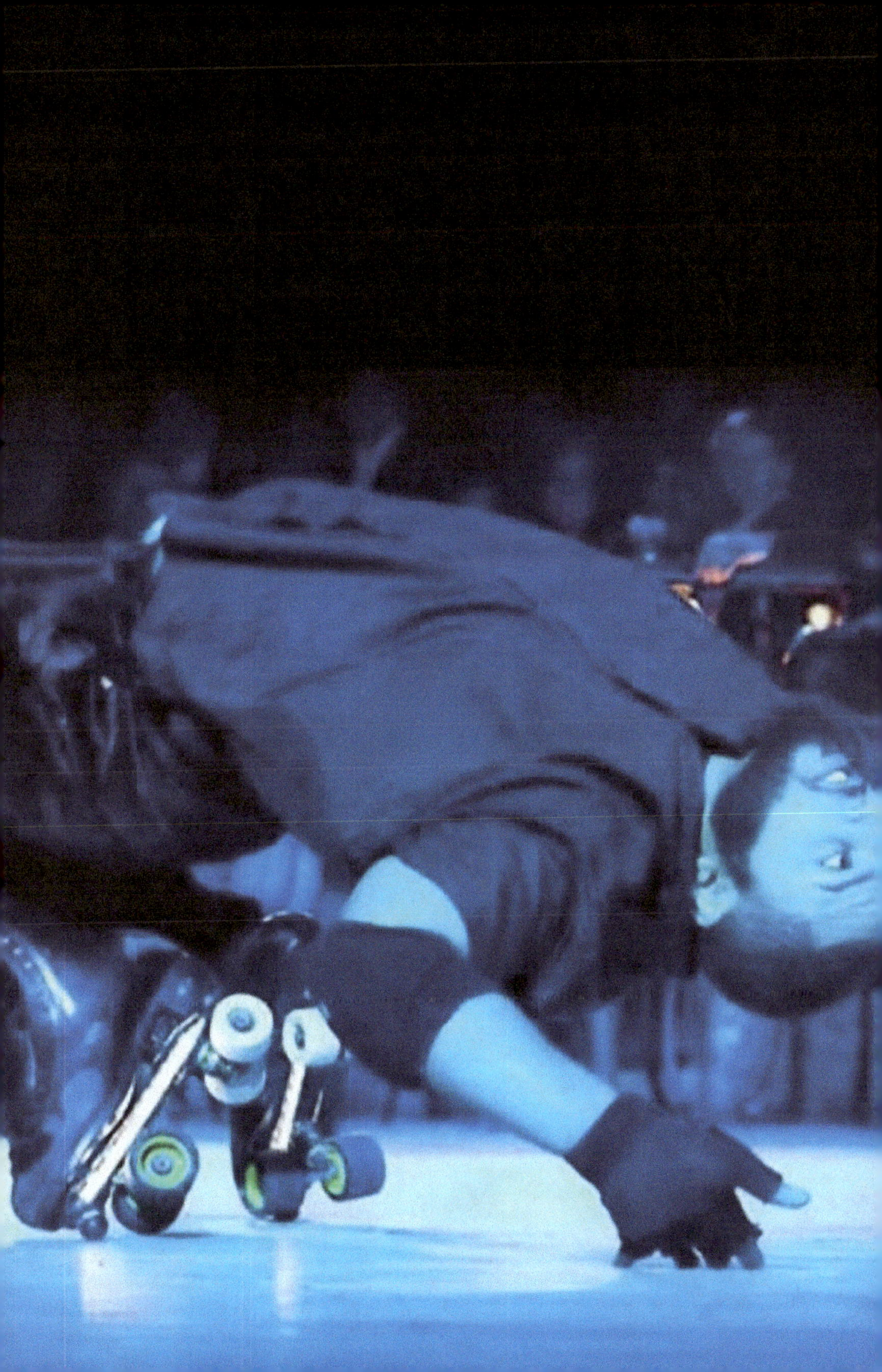

continue pushing the art forward. I'm standing on the shoulders of giants who preceded me. I must do my part. I'm here to promote love, unity, and peace. I'm here to help evolve and change the game for the benefit of the culture. I'm here because of God and Him alone. I'm here to raise the bar and then help the next generation make it farther.

I must be the change. If we need more love in our community then I'll show more love. If we need help, I'll be the help.

God is over all so I'll give it all. God save my soul. Skating saved my life. What are you here for?

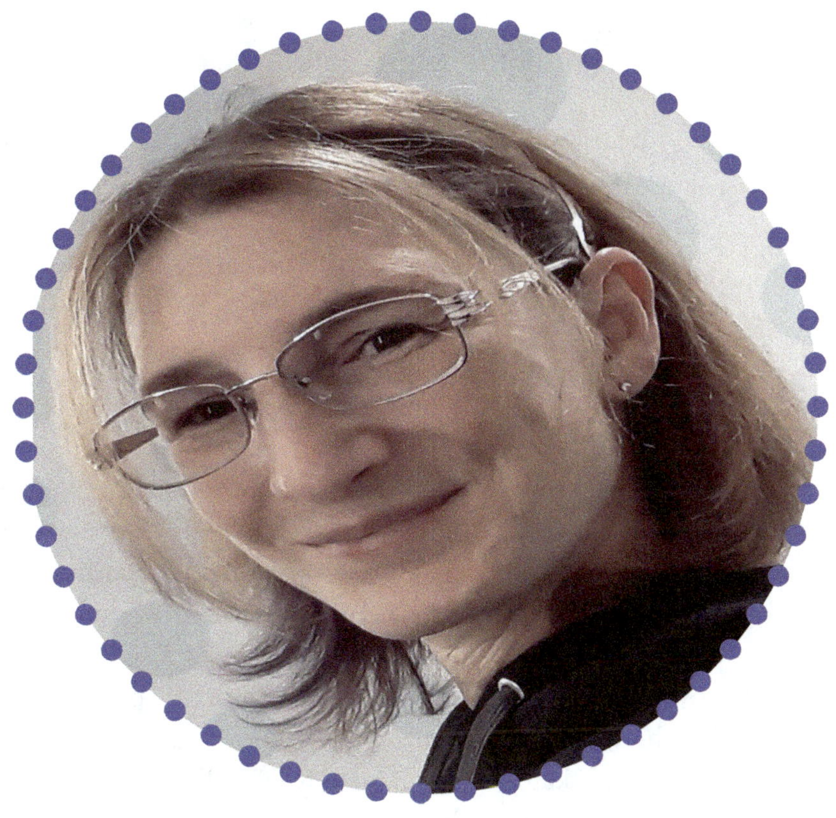

Ramona Guy

aka Snowflake

Facebook: @Ramona Guy | Instagram: @ramonzie77

"She Be Rollin'"

Let me introduce myself...Ramona Guy, aka Snowflake! I was born and raised in Germany. I am a daughter, sister, wife of twenty-two years, and mother of two boys! My chosen career field in dentistry has spanned some twenty-seven wonderful years—while residing in the USA for twenty-one of those years.

Here is how my journey started. We had a boy scout outing at the local rink in Wichita, Kansas, and well, that's where it all began in 2009! Our whole crew would skate every Wednesday with the boys and me for cheapskate, as it kept them out of trouble. One day, another roller skater, tripped my son on the skate floor, and that's how I met my best friend and skate partner—Rhamija. He's a smooth-rolling JB Style skater we would always look up to. We rolled together every week, starting from barely being able to stand on brownies—to backward skating. Our boys started speed skating. The youngest started competing, watching YouTube videos, and admiring the amazing skill that everyone had.

The Rich Boys had me hooked and many others inspired me. I wanted to be part of this community! I love skating! It's so much fun seeing all those smiles!

Dancing is also one of my loves, so I knew this was something I wanted to pursue. Rolling on those 8's became addictive. Finding the kind of environment for the skating I saw in videos—was difficult. The rink was there, but adult skating disappeared altogether in Wichita many years ago. Starting skating with no confidence on rentals—to

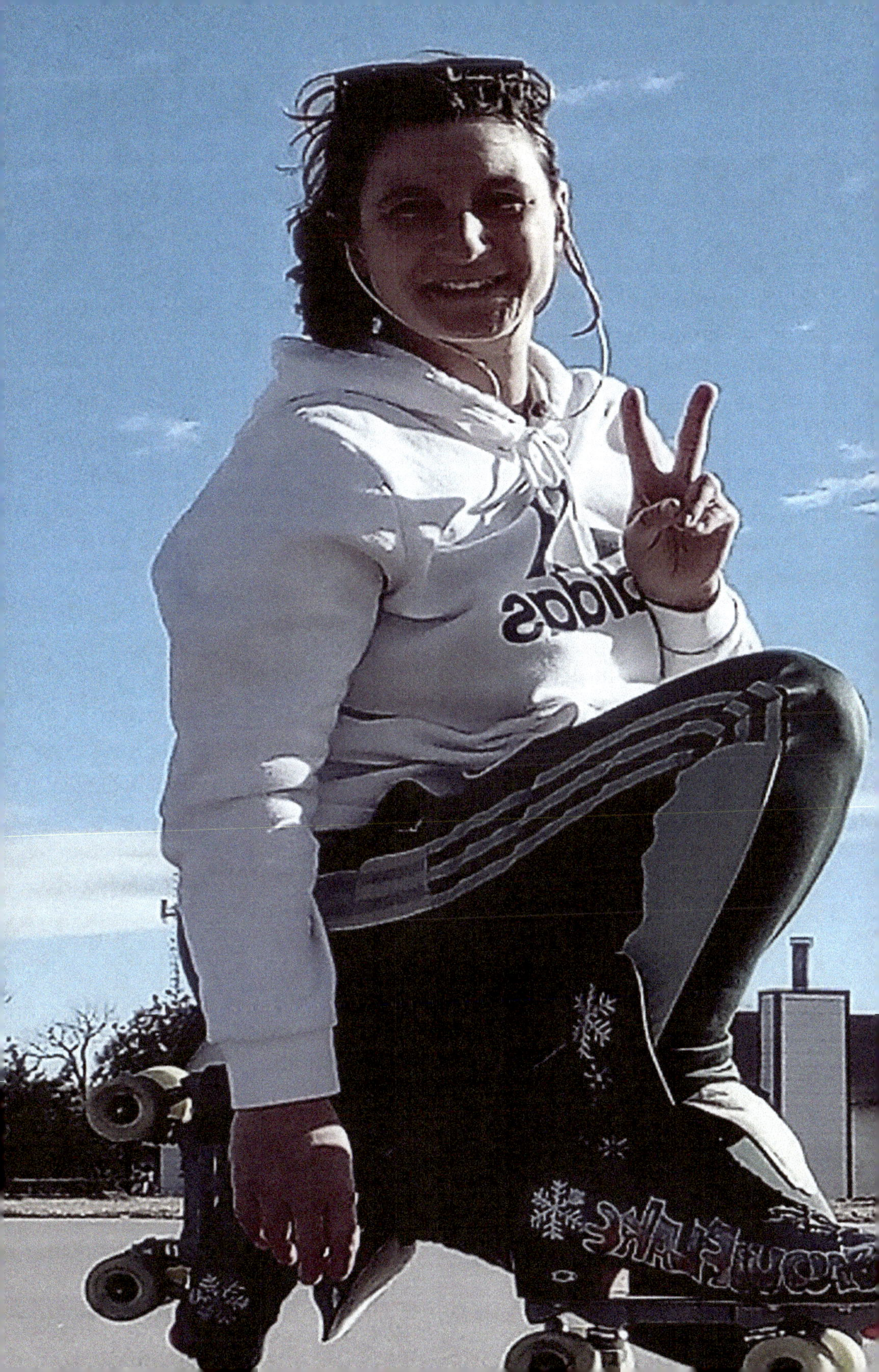

buying my first GTX skates, then first high-top boots, and joining a small group of younger roller skaters—moved my confidence forward. But, going to Winnwood Skate Center around 2010 in Kansas City for the 'Summer Skate Jam' in August every year— intimidated.

Despite the fear of possible performance anxiety at such an event, we were all welcomed with open arms. We met Susie Anderson, CdMan and DJ Soul Train, and DJ Bowen—who graciously invited us to other skate parties like "OKC SoulRoll," where we met Odis Rowlett. All of this received skate community love—encouraged my going to more skate parties with everyone in the group. We had the determination to put Wichita Kansas, back on the map in the skate community. As time went on, our group gained more skaters who wanted to travel every day—so I upgraded to OG 172 skates.

Thanks to Facebook, I have met and remained in touch with a lot of wonderful skaters. Now, I have been able to meet most of them face to face—and I call them my skate family and friends. I attended my first big skate party in 2018, the Dallas Skate Fair Classics. It was such a great experience; I loved every minute of it—so I had to come back for more! Learning new skills, meeting new people, and especially line dances—this is what continues to bring me back to the skate world time after time. Skating is almost like a drug to me—I have to have it in my life. The name SNOWFLAKE was a funny gift to me by my best friend—and it stuck!

The first time I let loose on skates, it popped out of his mouth.

He said, "Snowflake…COLD as ICE!"

We just rolled with it! I learned the crazy legs from Richard Humphrey videos and can't wait to meet him maybe one day in person. So much to learn.

I don't have a favorite skate style, but if I had to pick—JB is probably my favorite style of skating. Why? Well, it was as they say—love at first sight. Smooth and controlled, that's my goal. Learning ballroom from Leo, which I have watched for years—improved my skillset. One of my favorite female skaters—Ebony (there are many others)—inspired me to BE more and BE myself! For a while, we tried getting a group together, but it never really worked out.

In late 2019, I believe, some of us started dressing in the same shirts, etc., doing the same moves in a line, inspired by what we saw while traveling. And Boom! THE SK8DEEZ was born! We had a few women wanting to get together and start skating for causes, like preventing suicide, Alzheimer's, breast cancer and we ended up on the *Good Morning Kansas Show* in late September 2019. We are women of all traits, skill levels, races, religions, and backgrounds—supporting each other in this crazy world—getting together on adult skate night. Thankfully, we have had an adult skate night at the Carousel Skate Center for a few years now. And with a short break after COVID-19, skating is back on a roll. We enjoy our friends visiting from OKC and Tulsa Skate Masters—and on those nights, a breath of fresh air and moves ensue!

During the pandemic, while finding a way to supplement income, I decided to put becoming a national group fitness and Zumba instructor on my agenda. Outdoor skating with friends was keeping everyone on 8's, fit, sane, and practicing new moves. It kept the excitement around helping us stay connected, learning tricks, and sometimes doing virtual sessions with other skaters from around the world. Thanks to the pandemic, I was able to become more confident on skates. Learning how to dip and slow things down for control—was something I never thought I would be able to accomplish. Roller skating has helped overcome: the grieving process of two best friends that passed in 2014/15 way before their time to breast/lung cancer. When homesickness strikes or a bad day comes along—skating helps you forget everything. Getting lost in the music and good vibes, letting everything roll off on the skate floor—*is priceless!*

People have called ME the life of the party—cheering everyone on while cheering them up. Life is too short! Sometimes you just got to *roll with it!* I always have love to give to everyone—along with a smile and a hug. Let's be real, we all need hugs!! My Goals: learning new things, encouraging others to have fun—and last but certainly not least—putting Wichita back on the skate map! We are still here, we never left!! Let's all roll together, forgetting the hate and hard times. Let's keep living life by spreading joy and love—while rolling on eights!

When you see me, just say, "Hi!" I don't bite!

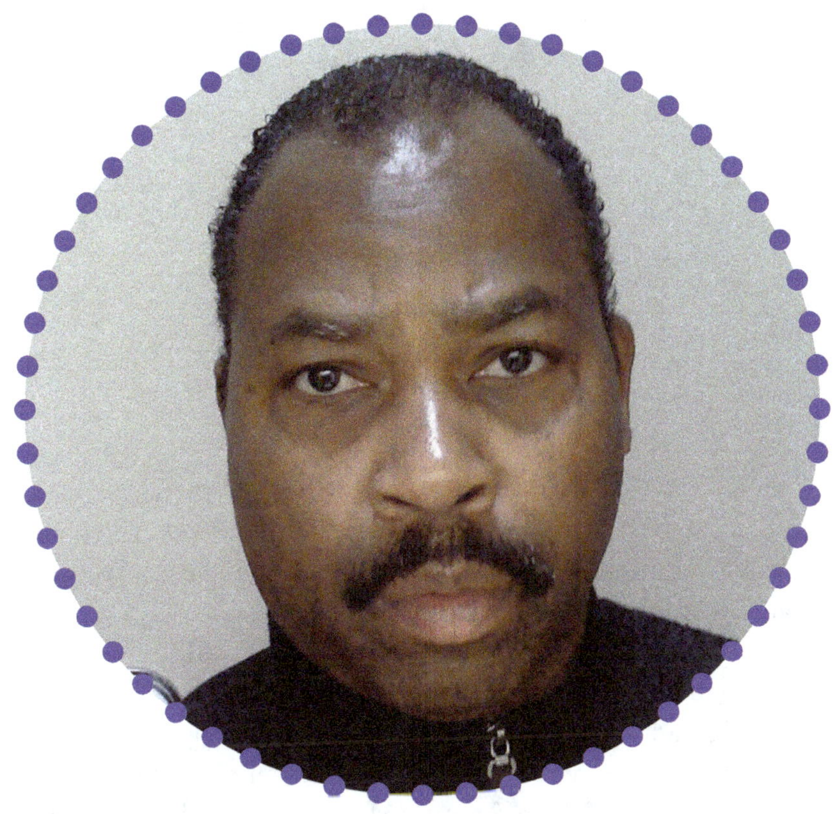

Richard Houston

aka CrazyLegs

Facebook: @Richard Houston | Instagram: @skateyourcase

"My Humble Beginning"

I was nine years old when I put on my first pair of metal roller skates I had gotten for Christmas. These skates had the tendency to vibrate my teeth out, but that didn't bother me! I strapped them over my shoes and skated on streets, sidewalks, parking lots, and even tried skating on grass or any other surface I could move on!

By the age of eleven, I had fallen in love with roller skating. It was 1974 when I had my first experience of roller skating in a gym, on a basketball court! The gym was inside the Lawrence Street Recreation Center, which was in North Atlanta/Marietta, Georgia. The first time I skated at the Center, it was so crowded I could barely get on the floor to skate. The basketball floor was rubber, so trying to skate on it was like skating in quicksand, and if you fell, you would end up with a nasty bruise or abrasion. We never complained because it was all we had to skate on, and we had one of the best DJs from Marietta to all over Atlanta. He remains one of the top DJs in Atlanta's nightlife. Considering that Blacks were not welcome to skate in any of the roller skating rinks back then, we made do with the hand we were dealt. Many of the new generations of skaters don't know where we have come from. If they did, there would likely be more support within the skating communities across the US, instead of the division that exists.

It was the last weekend of Summer 1976 when I stepped into my first skating rink experience after my girlfriend had been trying to convince me the entire summer. I cut my skating teeth at South Cobb Skating Rink, later to be named Sparkles Smyrna.

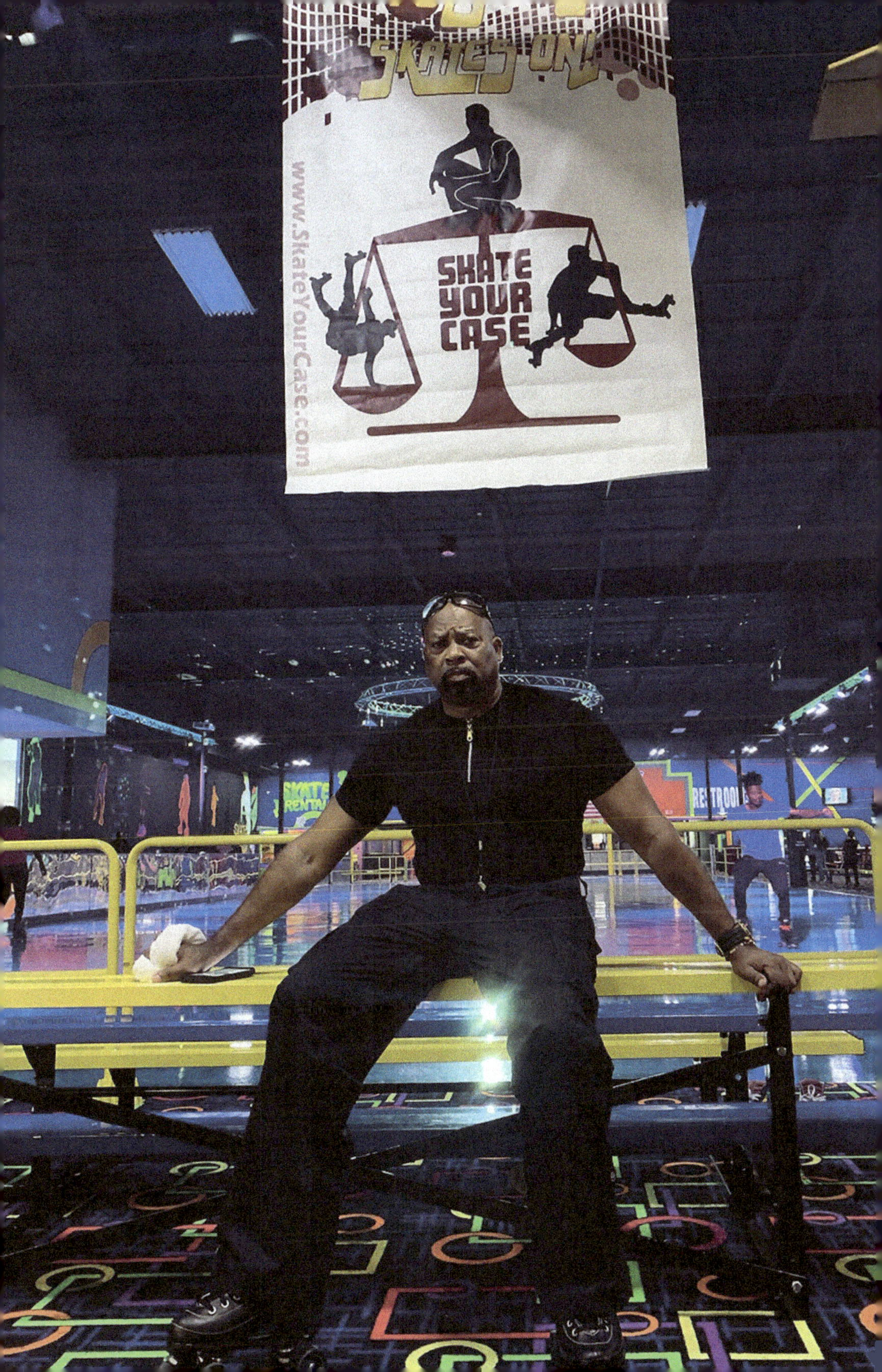
SKATES ON!
www.SkateYourCase.com
SKATE
YOUR
CASE

I will never forget the first time going around the rink, which took me about five minutes because I fell so many times that I lost count, but my derriere didn't! My girlfriend didn't help any, making matters worse by laughing and shouting at me, "I thought you could skate." She screamed at the top of her lungs, ridiculing me.

I was born with a competitive spirit and would not give up. I looked at her and shouted, "You are laughing at me now, but give me a few months, and I will be turning this rink out," as I skated around the rink, channeling Fred Sanford's walk on wheels! I fell again at the turn.

She skated up and looked down at me, and siad, "Yeah, turning it out on your behind!"

I was hellbent, with my focus on learning how to skate, so I started going skating three times a week.

My friends were in the beginning stages of roller skating also, so we all went to different rinks during the week. We skated at Skatetowne off Old National on Tuesday nights, Cascade, or Big Shanty, which became Sparkles Kennesaw, on Wednesdays. As the weeks of learning passed, I was getting better and had gained my confidence on my wheels!

It was 1977 when I entered my first roller skating competition. By then, I had developed into my very own style, unique to all the other skaters on the Atlanta skating scene.

I remember times when I would skate around the rink, and I could hear many of the skaters say under their breaths, "I don't know what that crazy stuff is that he is doing, but it ain't skating! It looks flicted to me, and it does not look natural! How does he do his legs like that? Look at him! He needs to sit down somewhere!"

I was sitting in the middle of the skating floor, doing my stretching exercises, just before my first competition. I stood and started doing a Crane Stretch, and while doing so, an older gentleman skated over to me and said, "Hello, young man. I've been watching you skate tonight, and you have a skate style. Where did you learn it from?"

"I taught myself. I watched all the other skaters, and all of them skate alike, so I developed my very own style, to be different."

"It is very different. That stretch that you are doing is called the Crane Stretch. Do you study martial arts?"

I studied Tae Kwon Do, so I was very limber back then. I told him, "Yes."

He then asked me if I had a nickname for my skating style, and I told him I didn't have a clue.

He said, "Good, because I have one for you. CrazyLegz Crane! I don't know what you are doing on your skates, but keep on doing it, because you've got a patent on that!"

At that very moment, CrazyLegz Crane was in full effect. That name has stuck with me since, among other names I had been called by my competition, because they hated to compete against me, telling me it was not fair for me to be in the competition because I knew I was going to win! All they had to do was practice as hard as I did—skating three days a week, to improve my style. I won my very first competition that night, and if you would have asked me how I did it, I didn't have any idea.

I went on with my winning ways for twelve years, being undefeated in every competition I competed in. During my skating era, I had grown up skating at just about every rink that I could pronounce, from all the Sparkles locations, Cascade, Golden Glide, Ben Hill, Skatetowne, and the historic JellyBeans, which is noted as the top Atlanta skating rink of all time. Everyone who had the chance to skate there knows it was a great experience. We all hated to see it go, especially knowing there was nothing we could do about it. We all were so young and didn't have a clue about what was going on. That is another story for another time and place.

Before I started competing in skating competitions, I was a dancer in one of Atlanta's top dancing groups: The Street Gang Dancers, which is now considered one of Atlanta's legendary dance groups. Yes, I am a dancer, too! I must show my dance crew some love. I must represent, so I give a big shout-out to my big brother and founding member/DJ, Greg Daniel, who is one of Atlanta's own legendary DJs. He is one of the original DJs of Sparkles Smyrna, Kennesaw, and Hiram. Also, the other members are Mervin Daniel, Shawn Williams, Harold McMurty, Tommy Milton, and the late Paul Kelly. My dancing roots have been the most integral part of my skating style from the beginning, during my competition days.

I was sixteen years old when the movie, *Skatetown USA*, came out. During the time the movie was out, I had a few skating competition trophies under my belt. I had the chance to see the movie and felt that I could have been in that movie because I could skate like the skaters in it!

In 1980, I had met this guy at Sparkles Roller Rink by the name of Tommy Milton, who is now one of my best friends. He had been searching for me for two weeks because he was a classmate of the late Hollywood producer, Gene Fowler, Jr., who was scouting for talent in a few of the Atlanta skating rinks and high schools. He had been searching for a particular skater and was unsuccessful in finding this skater.

This was the description my friend Tommy gave me from the comment that he had heard from Gene Fowler, Jr.

Gene Fowler was getting frustrated because he was running out of time. "I have been in nearly every skating rink in Atlanta, and I have not had any luck in finding this skater! I know he skates in one of the rinks here in Atlanta, but nobody seems to know his name or have a phone number or where he lives. He is a young, skinny Black kid that wears blue jeans, with a red, white, and blue headband around his thigh, red, white, and blue wrist bands, with the same color headband on his head! He wears a black football jersey with the number 25, with red numbers, with the state of Texas on the back, with the craziest legs that you have ever seen on skates! The state of Texas was Houston," which was my last name.

I missed my chance of being in a skate movie!

I had envisioned the roller skating movement since film school. I am a film communications major from Clark/Atlanta University. I also have an Associate's in Fashion Merchandizing, Fashion Illustrations, Apparel Engineering, and Textiles. I have been a true fashionista since I was fifteen years old. I was a print model, runway, and mannequin model for Bohannon Enterprises in Atlanta in my younger days. I have done the Loew's Fashion Show, Rich's Fashionata Fashion Show, and GQ Live Atlanta in my fashion life, but when it's all said and done, I am still a skater, among many things that encompasses who I am.

I am a skater innovator and the producer of "Skate Your Case," a groundbreaking roller skating show on The CW17 Network in the Florida Market, streaming worldwide on various platforms. I started my vision with "Skate Your Case" in 2010 and launched the show in 2019. In 2020, the COVID-19 pandemic halted my production. In 2021, it was time to get back to business as usual. Therefore, Season 2 would launch on the CW17 Network in July 2021. I had plans to take the show International that year.

Yes, I see big things happening in the skate world. I will launch two clothing lines geared toward skaters, and I also have another television project in the works for our skate discipline or genre. I don't spend as much of my time skating as I used to because there is so much work to do to support the cause of a true skater. When you read about all the skaters, I hope you realize we are more than just people rolling around a rink, vibing to a funky beat. We are doctors, attorneys, nurses, IT directors, and just about any type of jobs and careers you could imagine.

My career is in telecommunications/television productions, but I am one of the top skaters in the history of Atlanta skaters. I even have my theme song: CrazyLegz's "Skate Anthem" on CD Baby, Spotify, and many more music streaming platforms. Imagine that! Therefore, with my history and legacy, I am motivated to take our roller skating culture to a level that many of us have never imagined. My goal is to ensure the so-called Underground Skater Movement that has overshadowed us for decades will be a thing of the past. Within my visionary skater journey, I am motivated to continue to make our discipline, genre, or style of skating in the history of urban culture a force to be reckoned with. I seek to get our skate culture the credibility and respect that our discipline deserves. Especially since beginning of social media, where every skater has somewhat of a platform. Many of them have an aura as if they are social media skating superstars, making any desperate attempt to grasp an ounce of notoriety to sell their soul at the cost of pennies on a dollar. Those that fall under this category should ask themselves: Where do I fit into the skate culture? Do they fit in as a "hater or skater" or "skater or innovator?"

On August 24, 2021, my hard work and dedication paid off when I was attended the Roller Skating Association (RSA) Convention in Tampa, Florida to showcase"Skate Your Case," to introduce it to many of the sponsors and rink owners that operate under RSA's criteria. They loved it!

Most importantly, I am now endorsed by RSA International for the future development of Urban Roller Skate Culture. Nothing like this has ever been done in our skate culture. Therefore, history has been made for Urban Skate Culture, and this is a new beginning for our movement. For the ones that don't understand this accomplishment, it has given us the notoriety and credibility that we have sought after for three decades.

I have a sanctioning body for our discipline, which will legitimize our roller skating styles and protect our vision by galvanizing our Urban Roller Skating Culture. I am going to do everything within my power to elevate our culture to a height that it has never been before, with various consortiums that I am developing within my production company: Elite Images Entertainment Group, Inc.

I am branding/developing my clothing line and another TV show under the "Skate Your Case" entity. I am also planning to go home to Atlanta to film my documentary of the Urban Atlanta Skate Culture, entitled: *Bring Your Skate Game: Rhythm of Our Souls*. The time is now to drop the underground moniker!

We had always been considered as "underground" roller skating, which I have always felt was an insult to our entire skating culture because we are over 39 million across the United States, and we are not going anywhere anytime soon because the "Rhythm Of Our Souls Is A Skater!"

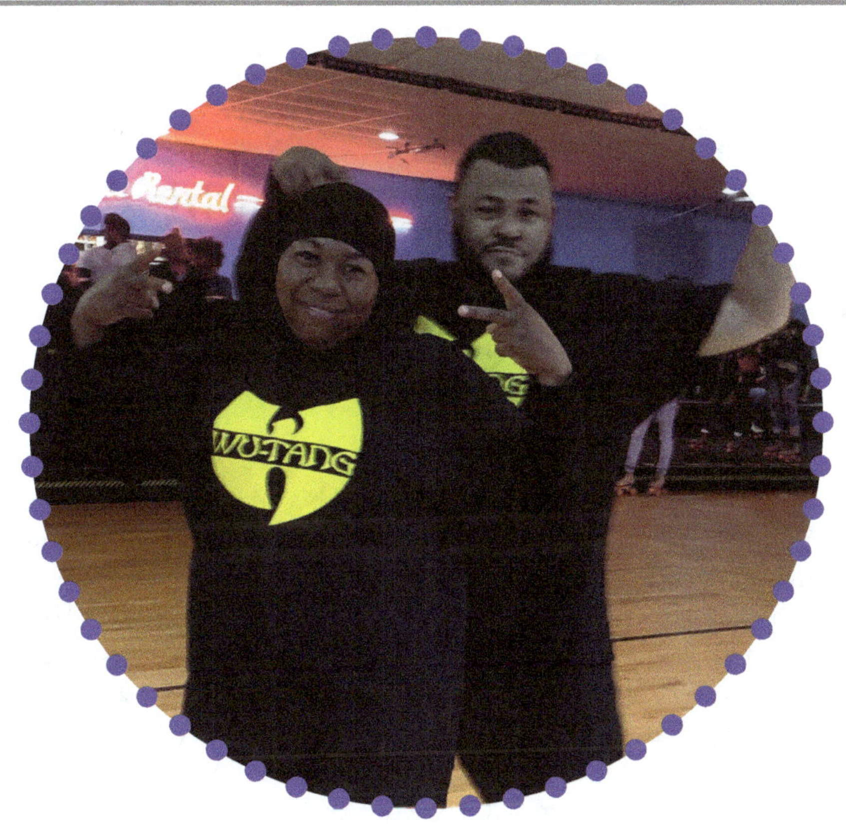

Wayne Tinsley, MBA
SeNequa Cade-Tinsley

aka Wayne & Mecka

Facebook: @Nassir_sharif | Instagram: @Nassir_sharif
Instagram: @Mecka_always

"Never Dim Your Light—Family Over Everything"

It all began when two college classmates became project partners in 1999 while attending college in Ann Arbor, Michigan. What started as being partners for a class project for a writing class—blossomed into friendship and eventually love. It was like we were meant to be. We built our friendship and dated throughout our college years. We had similar dreams and aspirations and knew that together we could be something special. One of the important things that we both wanted and talked about a lot was having a family in which we could create a legacy. After graduation in 2003, we decided to venture out—moving to Philadelphia to start our life's journey together.

Philadelphia welcomed us with warm arms and became a place where our family foundation started. Being exposed to so many types of people and cultures was an amazing eye-opener for us. The hustle and bustle of the city was a change of pace from what we grew up with and encountered in college. In 2003, We embraced Islam by taking our Shahada (Islamic declaration of faith) and developed a deep-rooted faith.

The Prophet Muhammad (peace and blessings be upon him) said, "He who marries has completed half his religion." Later that year and during the holy month of Ramadan, we married with a small ceremony.

In 2004, God blessed us with our first child, Jadah. Although Mecka and I helped raise our siblings, she was our introduction to true parenthood. A few years had passed, and it came a time where we decided to move back to the Midwest for a career move and advancement. Although we loved Philadelphia, we had to do what was

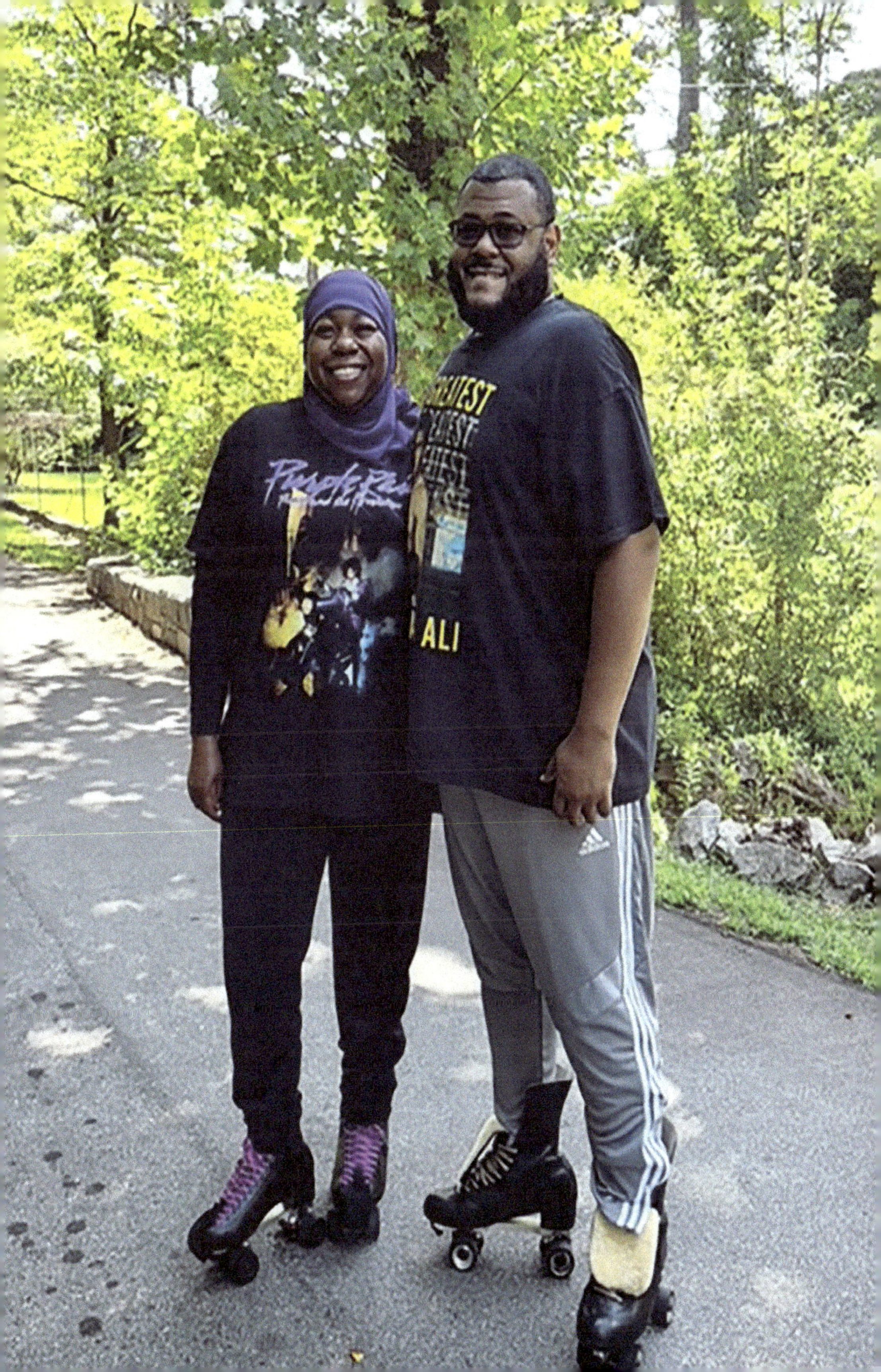
ALI

best for our family. In 2010 and after a six-year gap, our first son Haneef was born. In 2012, Muhammed followed. Finally, in 2014, Umar, who is our last child was born. Our dreams of having a family came true! After a four-year stint in Indiana, we had another career opportunity present itself and were off to Atlanta.

After moving to the Atlanta area, our family started skating more because we found ourselves settling into a happy place in our lives. Although we would skate from time to time as a fun activity, we could not fully enjoy ourselves because of limited rink access, not every family skated, and Mecka did not have comfortable skates. When we did go, it was to the family sessions at the rink that was closest to our home.

Fast forward to Skate-A-Thon 2017. We decided to have some 'grown-up' fun and attend our first major skate party. Having four relatively small children at the time, we did not get to enjoy many adult activities. At this event, we immersed ourselves in an introduction to a wide variety of complex skating styles within the culture. This event motivated us to learn more about the different styles and try to expand our range of movements on our skates. Our family began to widen our rink choices and started frequenting rinks that embraced and catered to more of what we wanted to perform on our skates. These rinks had more of a rink etiquette that limited interruptions during sessions and played music that the entire family could enjoy. During this time, one particular style grabbed our attention, "ATL STYLE!"

Shortly after attending Skate-A-Thon, we discovered a group of skaters that always seemed to be having fun and moving differently than the other skaters that were at the rinks. Sick on Skates Crew captivated the crowd and had an energy that electrified the building. At that moment we knew we wanted to learn that style. SOS Crew is a skating crew that specializes in the ATL Style of skating which is based on a dance style created in Atlanta and its surrounding areas now dubbed 'Yeeking.' However, being new to the ATL 'skate world' and experiencing some skaters being rude and putting us off—due to our newcomer status, or not having as much experience, or a certain look—all prevented us from being so quick to ask for help. We teach our children to always try and surround themselves with people who will not try to dim their light, but who will help enrich, nourish, and allow it to flourish. Following that mantra, there is no need to feel the need to change yourself to fit in with shallow people. That being said, we kept having fun and roller skating with our children. Our thoughts were when it was time, the right person or people would come along to help take us to the next level.

One day while we were out grabbing a bite to eat, a person tapped Mecka on the shoulder and asked if she was a skater.

Mecka turned and answered saying, "Yes and No."

Yes, because she loves to skate, and no, because she could not do all the fancy stuff like a lot of the skaters in Atlanta could. She then used him as an example because she had seen him skate before.

The man replied, "If you love to skate then you are a skater. It does not matter what tricks you can and cannot do on your skates. It's about enjoying yourself."

This led us introducing ourselves to one another. We learned that the man was Tony Sailor, the creator and founder of Sick on Skates Crew (SOS) which specializes in doing the style of skate we wanted to learn, ATL Style! That small encounter is what lead us to the next step in our journey. Tony's knowledge of Atlanta skate history is vast, and his love for the ATL skating culture is contagious. Tony with his inspiration quickly transformed into a skate mentor and coach. He and his family have become special friends to the Tinsley's.

In Mecka's Words...

I grew up roller skating with my family and friends. So, when I think of skating, I always think of family/community fun first. As young as I can remember it was always something I and many other people within my community did with family or friends. I can remember being as young as four- or five-years old flying around Link's Roller Rink (no longer operating) with my family doing what we called a train. We would all skate in a single file line, sometimes holding the leading person's shirt, hand, or shoulder going fast with all of us doing the same movement on our skates. I skated almost daily, whether it was indoors or outdoors, and sometimes both. Some of my best childhood memories revolve around roller skating with family and friends. It was not until my family moved to another state and we did not have a skating rink nearby that I stopped roller skating regularly as a teen. However, whenever I would travel back home for a visit, I always would rush to my old childhood rink that was still open at the time—Roller Dome South.

As I grew older and transitioned into adulthood, I occasionally skated but never found the time to fully rekindle my passion for it. However, once I became a parent, I knew I wanted to introduce roller skating to my children because it had been such an integral part of my childhood. Roller skating offered me numerous mental and physical health benefits—it was a source of calmness during moments of anger, a reason to smile when feeling sad, and a belief that I could achieve anything in life. Moreover, it provided a full-body workout and served as a positive outlet and coping mechanism for me.

As my husband and I started our family, I made an effort to take our children to the nearest roller rink as often as possible, typically around the age of three—the same age I began roller skating. I taught my children to skate without any assists, encouraging them to slow down their wheels until they felt comfortable moving faster. However, this became challenging as my husband, Wayne, didn't skate at all, unlike me who grew up with roller skating as a regular activity. Consequently, I found myself supervising several beginners while dealing with the discomfort caused by poorly maintained rental skates.

I soon realized that not all rinks took good care of their rental skates, and my childhood resilience didn't quite carry over into adulthood. As a result, we only visited the rink on special occasions like school fundraisers or celebrations over the next few years.

After relocating to Georgia, my desire to share my love for skating with my family began to materialize. Fortunately, Georgia boasts several roller rinks, most of which offer affordable prices for families, making it easier for us to visit regularly. To my surprise, my husband gifted me my own pair of skates for our 14th wedding anniversary. This thoughtful gesture eventually led to us buying skates for our entire family—including our four children and, finally, my husband!

Acquiring roller skates for my husband was a significant milestone. Since he didn't grow up roller skating, it wasn't initially a part of his regular routine. He typically watched me skate with our family and friends over the years. So, when he expressed an interest in getting his own pair, I wasted no time in getting them for him before he changed his mind! This marked the beginning of our journey as a roller-skating family and made it easier for me to uphold my passion and family tradition.

Along the way, I met Tony Sailor, the creator of Sick on Skates Crew (SOS) that specializes in the ATL Style of skating. Meeting Tony, and eventually joining SOS, not only helped to take my skating abilities to another level but also allows me to teach and expose my children to different degrees of excellence inside and outside of the rink. The Atlanta area has so many talented dancers and skaters from different origins. It allows myself and my children to be exposed to much more complicated and difficult moves than I could ever think of trying on my skates.

Finally, being able to pass down roller skating to my children as I always wanted fills me with so much joy. I get to witness firsthand how it has helped them become more independent, fearless, and self-confident—not just in their skating, but in all aspects of their lives. Successfully giving them something that not only provides tremendous physical health benefits, without them even realizing they're exercising, but also serves as a positive outlet to help them cope with life stresses, brings me immense satisfaction.

I love how roller skating has provided my family and me with another way to connect and maintain our strong bond. Now that roller skating is back in my life, I can't imagine ever giving it up. Eventually becoming one of the skating rink's elders seems like a probable future for me. By continuing to assist the younger generations, I hope to pass down a legacy to any future grandchildren I may have!

In Wayne's Words…

I wasn't a skater until 2017. Prior to that, I had only skated three times in my entire life. Whenever we went skating before that, I would either sit on the sidelines and watch or play video games at the rink. I didn't grow up skating and never had much interest in it. In the area of Virginia where I grew up, there weren't many black people, and the closest rink was located in a predominantly white area. In my mind, skating was something that white folks did for fun. However, when Mecka and I got together and she expressed her interest in skating, I decided to give it a try because I wanted to spend time with her and engage in activities she enjoyed. It made sense to me that she enjoyed skating, considering she grew up in Indiana. It was only later that I discovered skating was a significant part of the Black community.

Once we had our kids, skating became a family activity. Despite my reluctance to join them on the floor, they eagerly wanted me out there with them. I would come up with every excuse to avoid trying until one day, while at the rink, Mecka surprised me with a pair of skates. That act of kindness marked the beginning of my skate journey. Our youngest son, Umar, and I started skating around the same time. He was just turning three years old, and I was thirty-eight. Hand in hand, he and I became skate partners, shuffling slowly around the rink. Meanwhile, Mecka was shaking off the rust, and our other kids were discovering the joy of skating. With the family's encouragement, Umar and I pushed ourselves out of our comfort zones. Mecka has a remarkable way of teaching things that resonate with our kids and me. They share her knack for quickly grasping skate concepts, whereas I struggle a bit more.

I'll be honest, the first few months in skates weren't as enjoyable as I expected. Learning how to skate is and continues to be a process. Everyone around me made it look effortless, which added to the pressure. But I realized I had to focus on my own progress and not compare myself to others. Being someone who enjoys challenges, and seeing how much my family loved roller skating, I committed to sticking with it, knowing I could only improve with time. Anxiety on the rink was a constant companion; I worried about falling, obstructing others, and looking awkward. However, my wife and kids were always supportive, cheering me on every step of the way. Their encouragement fueled my determination to keep going. In a way, they were teaching me more about skating than I was teaching them. They saw their dad and husband setting goals and working hard to achieve them, which is not just a skate lesson but also a life lesson.

After several months of consistent trips to the rink, things started to get more comfortable. Adult nights with the wife and family sessions with the kids became something I was looking forward to.

When I let go of the anxiety and just had fun, it then became fun. My perspective changed, and I looked at skating differently. The way I heard music changed. I developed a 'skater's ear' for songs I feel I could skate to in confidence. When I watched other skaters, I could see their technique and started to understand what they were doing. In the learning process—my appreciation for the different styles and skaters grew more. Developing a passion for skating has truly grown within me—and sometimes I regret not starting sooner in life. However, I was not exposed to it therefore it did not resonate with me. Everything happens for a reason.

Up to this point, I had not had a teacher for skating other than my talented wife who has been skating since she was a kid. She has always been my favorite skater and will always be. Besides her, another major influence has been Tony Sailor. Fast forward to 2019, after trusting the process and learning with Sick on Skates Crew, my wife and I became members of the SOS Family. To me, being a part of this team surpasses what I set myself out to accomplish with skating. I feel honored and proud to be a part of this extended family and legacy. The team's purpose and mission fall in line with our beliefs and values.

T-Clan Skates: The Future

T-Clan Skates was formed to promote positivity and share moments in our family's life that inspire others. We decided to create this to show that the family unit and structure are imperative, important, and to support the dreams and aspirations collectively and individually of the Tinsley family. Our skate journey has been amazing so far. What started as wanting to skate to spend quality time with my family and re-establishing a family tradition has flourished into being part of our story. Creating memories and cherishing the time together with family and friends is the most important aspect of skating for us. Sometimes it is surreal how far our family has come, and we are looking to what is to come in the future.

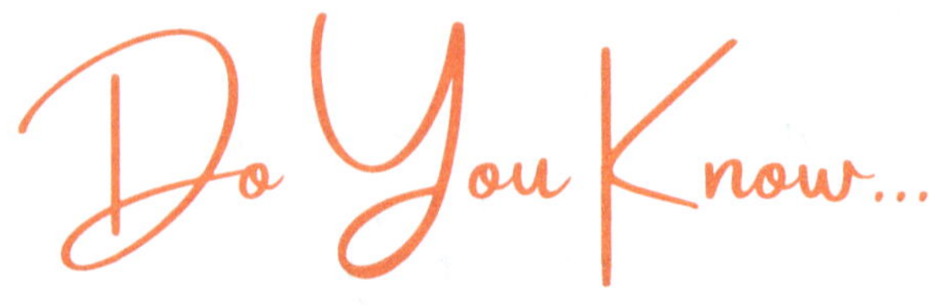

About the Oldest Rink the U.S.?

The Oaks Park Skating Rink, situated in Portland, Oregon, holds the distinction of being the oldest operational roller rink in the U.S. It stands as a historical landmark and a symbol of communal joy.

Opening its doors on May 30, 1905, the rink has weathered significant challenges throughout its history, including the Great Depression, the 2008 recession, and, most recently, the COVID-19 pandemic.

Boasting the second-largest skate floor in the country, measuring 20,000 square feet of skateable surface, it remains a popular destination for roller skating enthusiasts.

Additionally, it proudly maintains the tradition of featuring a live pipe organ, making it the last roller rink with this unique feature in operation.

Over the years, the rink has garnered attention in the entertainment industry, having been featured in various movies and TV shows, including *Free Willy*, *Leverage*, *Breaking In*, *Untraceable*, *Portlandia*, and *Grimm*.

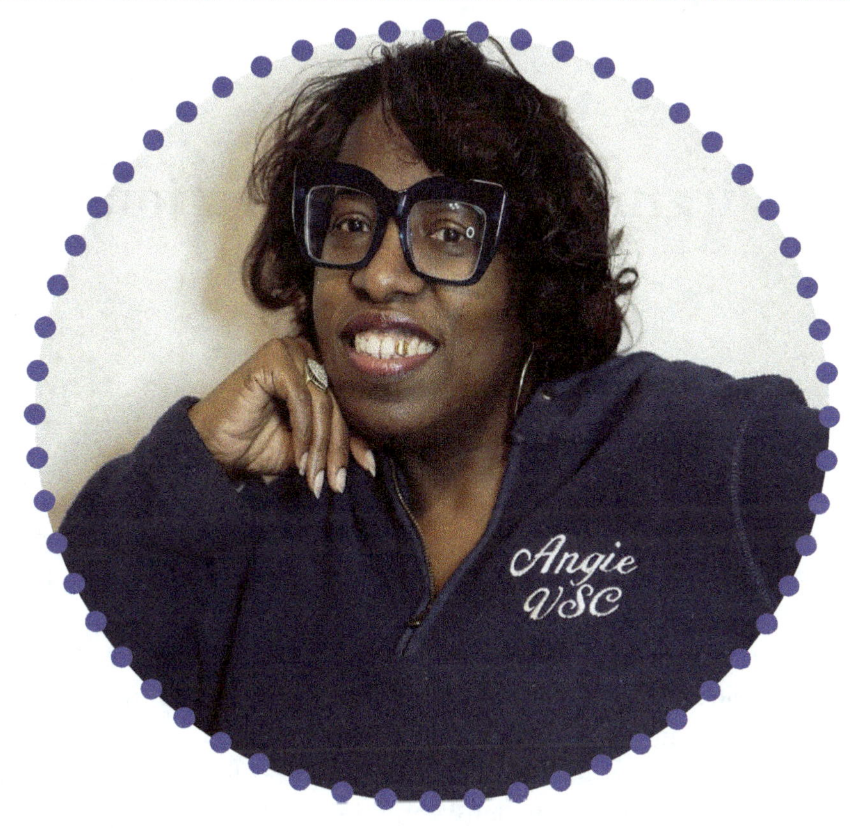

Angela Parham

aka My Sk8ts

Facebook: @Angela Anita Parham

"Virginia Skate Connection"

I was born and raised in Richmond, Virginia, and I've been skating for fifty years. Respectfully known in the skate community as Momma Angie and Ms. Angie, I started at age five during a time when most kids received bicycles and roller skates for Christmas. Growing up, I skated on sidewalks throughout our neighborhoods, linking up with other kids at designated houses to skate up and down hills and circles until we decided to head to our recreation center. Riding bicycles and roller-skating were our daily activities, making our way fun and challenging by stopping at each person's house along the route to ensure everyone joined our skate train, which lasted for hours. Those were truly the good old days.

As the years passed, I continued to cherish my love for skating as a teenager, young adult, and now, after fifty years of rolling, I consider myself a seasoned skater. Throughout my journey, I explored various rinks in Virginia, often attending Sunday and Monday night adult roller skating sessions hosted by our local DJ Kirby Carmichael at Skateland and Cavalier Skate Center. DJs like Fish, Captain Fresh (John Rozzell), Disco T (Tolliver Carpenter), and Kirby Carmichael Jr. made those sessions addictive, and missing one was out of the question as they became the hotspot for our adult community to gather and skate.

With a strong passion for roller skating, I, along with a group of local skaters, joined the Richmond Soul Rollers and later founded

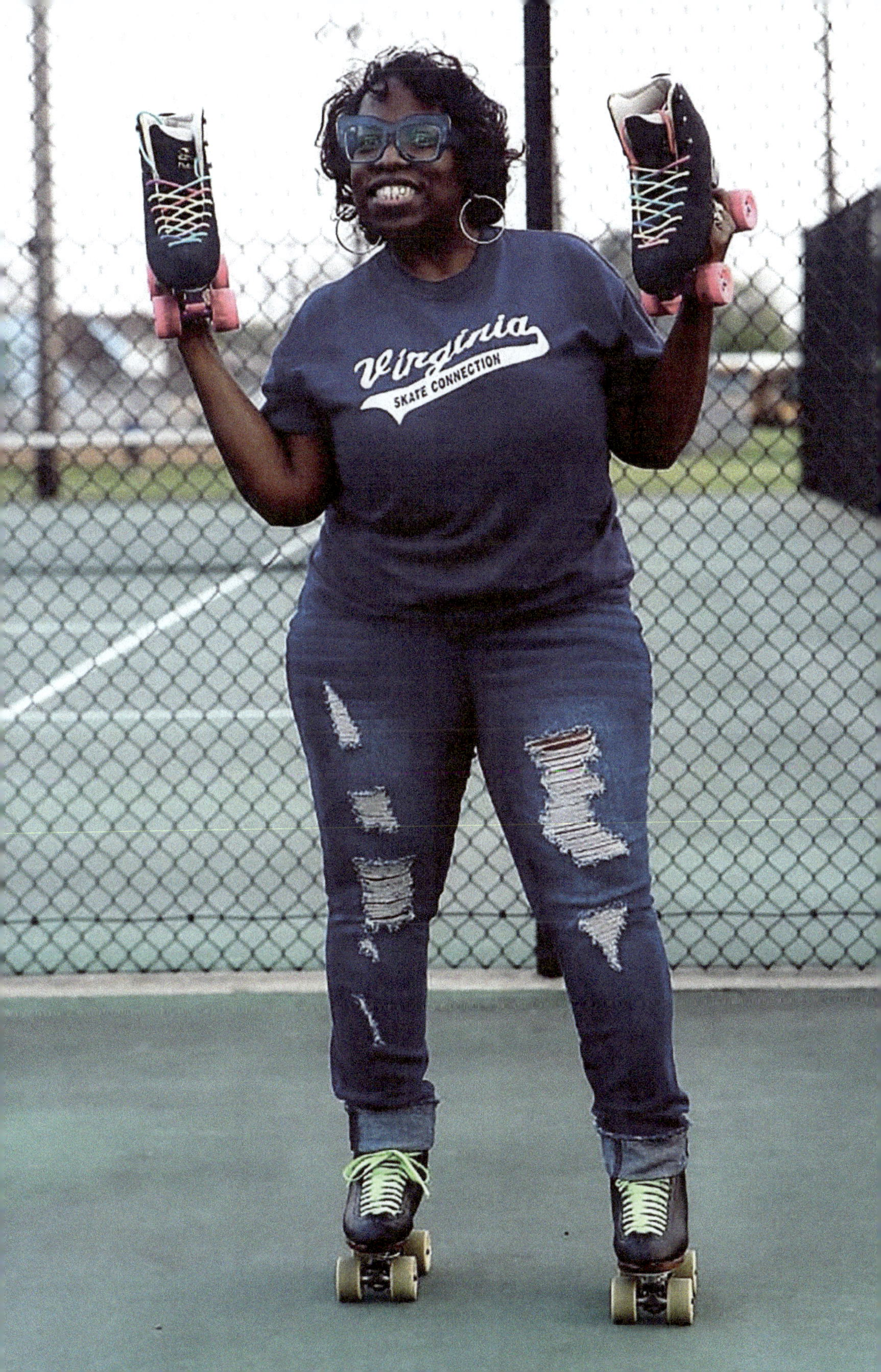
Virginia
SKATE CONNECTION

VSC (Virginia Skate Connection) in September 1999. Witnessing a group of responsible and dedicated skaters come together to motivate and encourage one another for the love of skating was a pleasure. Together, we built a supportive and cohesive team that served our adult community from 1999 to 2019, celebrating our 20th Anniversary on September 21, 2019.

Our journey with VSC garnered love and respect from skaters locally, nationally, and internationally. Traveling allowed us to form bonds with skaters who have since passed away and learn from legends who continue to share their knowledge and experience. I owe a debt of gratitude to three skaters and leaders, Desi Crawl (Skategroove.com), Nikki Robinson (CEO & President at Style Skaters Television Network), and Khannie Butler (TheScenario), who mentored me in hosting adult roller skating events and helped me become the leader I am today.

Building VSC's reputation was a collective effort, especially with the infusion of young talent that brought passion and diversity to our team. We expanded our travels extensively, reaching states like Alabama, Kentucky, Ohio, Florida, and New York. Notable skaters like Mike (Diddy) Giles, Lawrence (Jit) Thomas, Sam Fonville, and Travis Swann joined us on our journey, representing Virginia Skate Connection positively and helping us establish strong connections within the skate community.

The reputation and integrity of VSC allowed us to collaborate with other skate organizations, such as Hoodtimes, leading to the creation of the All-Sweat Skate Weekend in Richmond, VA, from 2010 to 2017. Our collaboration brought together skaters from near and far, creating unforgettable memories and experiences.

One of the most rewarding collaborations was with Ms. Joi Loftin, known as Queen of the South, with whom I co-hosted the One Night Affair Regional Skate Event. Our goal was simple: to provide a night of skating without the frills—just pure skating enjoyment. Our first event held in Newport News, VA, was a testament to our vision, featuring DJs Big Man and Brian (Killa B) from Atlanta, GA.

Throughout my journey, I've had the privilege of collaborating with remarkable individuals like Joi Loftin and cherished friendships with skaters like Yvette L. Jones and Lashonda SkateDiva. Our friendship extends beyond skating, making us more than friends—we're family.

Skating has defined my life, providing a platform for caring, sharing knowledge, and fostering unity within our community. My proudest moment came from mentoring Angelica Jones, who has blossomed into a talented skater, DJ, photographer, videographer, and mother. Angelica embodies the spirit of my favorite quote: Always Lead by Example.

As I reflect on my roller skating journey, I cannot forget the adventurous trip we took during the snow blizzard to Elsmere Skating Rink in Delaware in 2003. Despite the challenges, we made it there safely and enjoyed an unforgettable weekend of skating, camaraderie, and fun, showcasing the true spirit of die-hard skaters.

Overall, roller skating has been more than a hobby—it's been a way of life, filled with love, passion, and devotion. And I wouldn't have it any other way.

Do You Know...

That Roller Skating Effects Your Mental Health?

The mental health benefits of roller skating are often overlooked, but we're here to shed light on how this simple activity can enhance your life by alleviating stress, aiding in weight management, and boosting self-confidence.

Stress plays a significant role in determining mental health outcomes. While stress is a natural part of modern life, it's crucial to find ways to unwind and actively engage in stress-reducing activities. Roller skating serves as an excellent stress-reliever. When you put on a pair of skates, especially as a beginner, your focus shifts from the source of stress to maintaining balance and stability. The smooth, gliding sensation of roller skating outdoors, with the breeze against your face, is a surefire way to reduce stress.

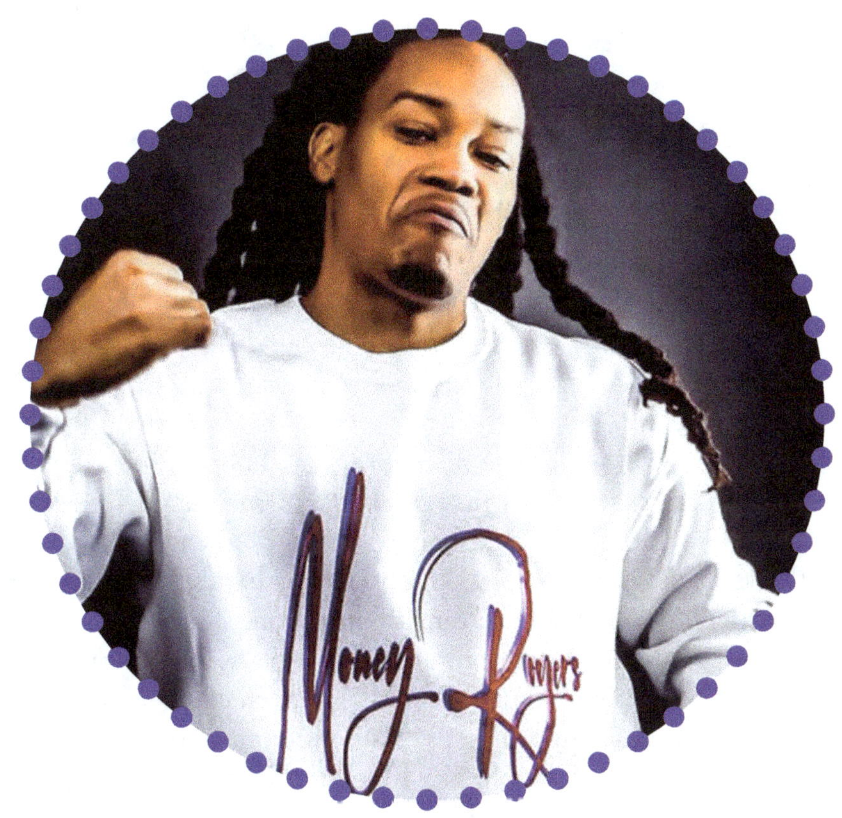

Jumaanee Rogers

aka 2 Smooth

Facebook: @Jumaanee Rogers | Instagram: @mrmoneyrogers

"The Humble Skater"

It all began at the tender age of four when I fell head over heels in love with roller skating. My first pair of skates were Pac-Man skates, and oh, how I adored them! Teaching myself to balance by clutching onto the kitchen sink, rolling back and forth marked the beginning of many kitchen roll-arounds. Transitioning from the kitchen floor to the outdoors was eye-opening; concrete proved a stark contrast to the forgiving kitchen floor, making each fall a new challenge. Despite the bumps and bruises, I found myself drawn even more to skating.

As the youngest of five siblings with a significant age gap, I enjoyed plenty of one-on-one time with my mother. With my older siblings more independent, my mother and I bonded over our regular trips to Rainbow Roller Rink on Chicago's North Side. This rink quickly became my second home, with its spacious floor, practice area, and game rooms—a young skater's paradise. By age eleven, I was hitting the rink three days a week, immersing myself in the vibrant skating culture.

Friday, Saturday, and Sunday nights meant piling into the car with friends for our skating escapades. During summer breaks, we took our skates to the nearby lakefront tennis court, skating until exhaustion set in. Life was simple then—school and skating were our main priorities, with worries melting away once our skates touched the floor.

Within a few short years, I gained recognition as one of the standout skaters among my peers. My friends and I formed a tight-knit skate group, complete with matching outfits and synchronized routines. Despite our collective efforts, I always aimed for a level of

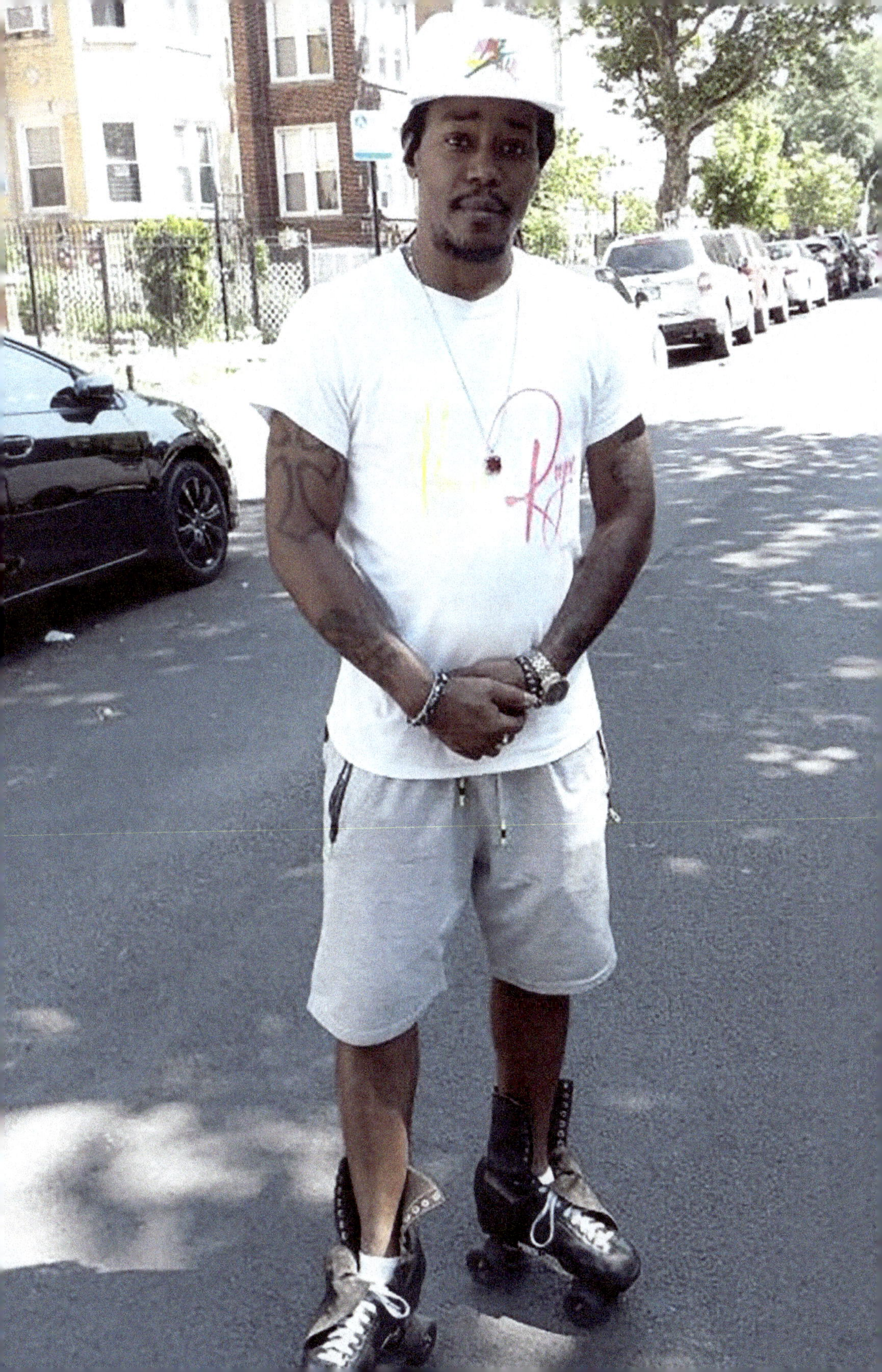

smoothness and finesse that set me apart. This pursuit of excellence stemmed from observing older skaters like DJ L7, whose effortless moves inspired me to strive for a similar gracefulness on wheels.

At fourteen, I seized the opportunity to showcase my skills in a teen skate competition. The prospect of winning the $150 prize fueled my determination, but an ill-timed attempt at a low shuffle resulted in a humbling fall, costing me the competition. It was a valuable lesson in humility and the importance of continuous improvement—an experience that would shape my approach to skating competitions in the years to come.

In the following years, my focus shifted briefly to Chicago's urban dance scene, known as "Foot Working." However, my passion for roller skating remained steadfast, and by seventeen, I was back on wheels for good. Sneaking into adult skate sessions became a regular occurrence, where my skills earned me respect among older skaters.

Venturing to the South Side of Chicago introduced me to a new skating community at Rink Fitness Factory on 87th Street. The vibrant energy and camaraderie drew me in, and I soon became a regular Sunday night skater. Reconnecting with old friends from my Rainbow Roller Rink days led to the formation of "Chi-Force Rollers," a skate group that would gain national recognition.

Over the years, Chi-Force Rollers grew in both size and reputation, winning awards at competitions and even appearing in commercials and TV shows. Roller skating became not just a hobby, but a way of life—a means of spreading joy and positivity. As skating rinks across the nation continue to close, I remain committed to sharing the transformative power of roller skating, especially in urban communities where it can provide hope and opportunity amidst adversity.

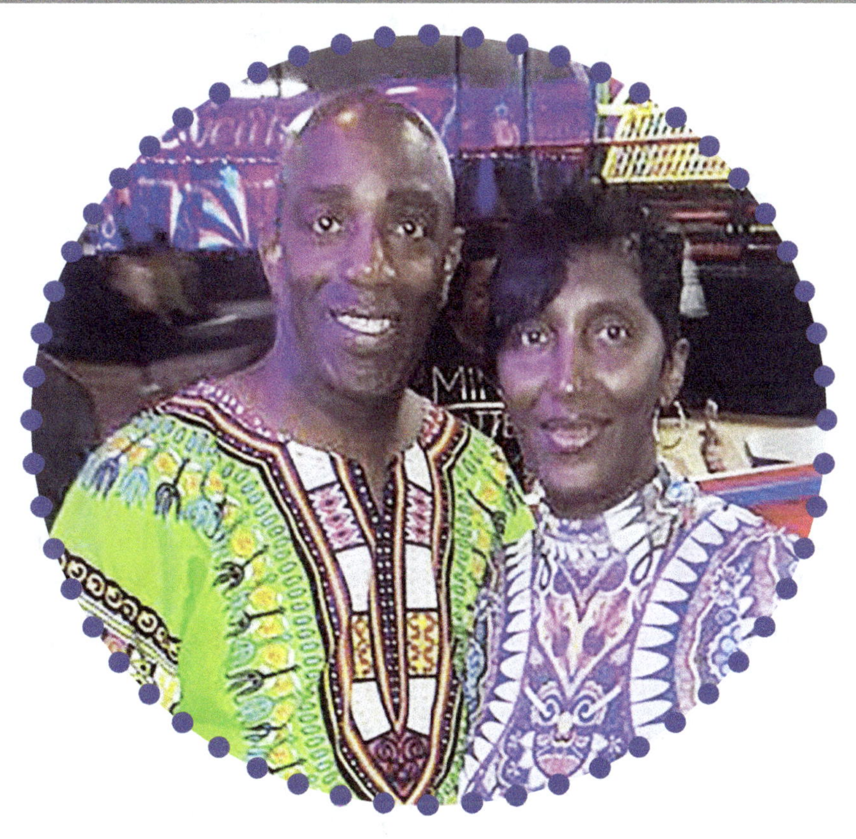

Tijuana & Kenneth Anderson

aka ATL Original Skaters

Facebook: @Kojak Anderson | Instagram: @lady_tee26

Facebook: @Tee Anderson

"OGs of Atlanta Skating"

Kojak (Kenneth Anderson) is a maintenance punch-tech man for an apartment complex and I (Tijuana Anderson) am a Retired Sales Rep for Delta Airlines.

Kojak was born in Atlanta, Georgia on August 26, 1961, and I was born on January 15, 1963, in Birmingham, Alabama. I moved to Atlanta Georgia and graduated from Therrell High School in 1981 and Kojak graduated from Sylvan High School in '79.

We were teenagers when we met at a local neighborhood skating rink in Atlanta, Georgia forty-one years ago. After six years of dating and roller skating together, we decided to get married because of the passion that we both had for roller skating. We later had our first child Deonta` who was a boy and Kojak was very excited about having a baby boy. A year and a half later we had another baby boy named De`Mario and this time Kojak was super excited! But now with the two boys and us still wanting to go roller skating created a situation. Yes, we needed a babysitter not just for one baby—but two. Kojak and I used every family member and friend that we could to babysit for us. Over the years, it started getting too expensive to pay the babysitters so we decided to start taking the boys with us.

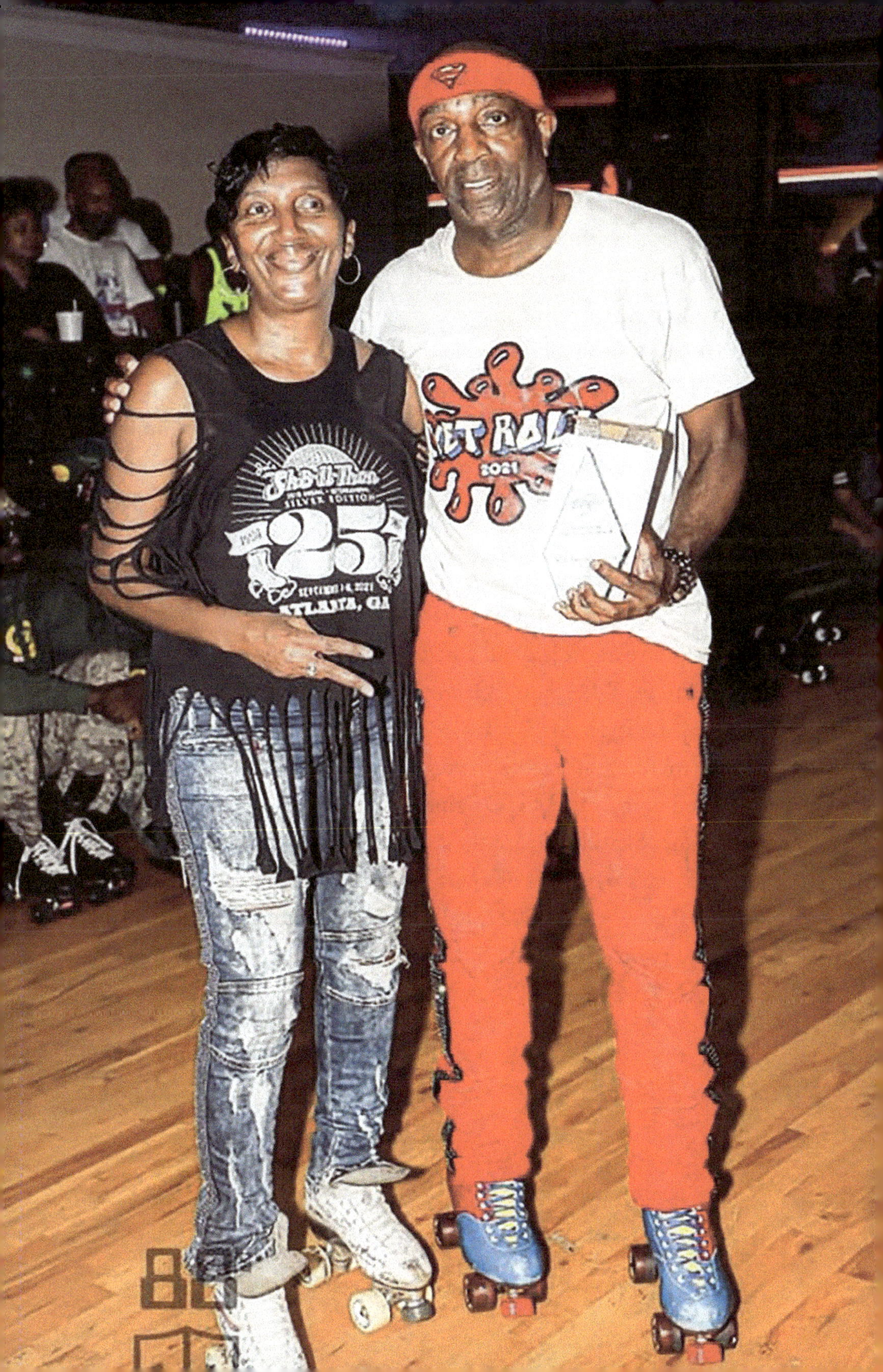
SILVER EDITION
25
ATLANTA, GA
2021

In the early '90s, the crowd grew bigger and bigger and the language of the skaters changed. So, we decided that we would no longer be able to take the boys with us until they got a little older. So, you know what that meant, back to the baby sitters drawing board again if we wanted to keep going skating. But that was okay because Kojak`s mom started to realize just how much roller skating meant to us and she decided to just watch the boys every skate night for us.

As the months and years went by—our skillsets as skaters improved with experience. The music was always great and the rink floor was immaculate! Teaming up with some of our friends—we started skating on another level. Eventually, we would compete against some of the other skaters in competitions. Believe it or not, we won 1st place in just about every competition we entered.

Over the years Kojak and I had become very popular in the skate world. We are the 'Atlanta Original Skaters,' known for our Hard-Core Skating Style. After years of roller skating, the two of us started traveling to different states showing off our ATL Skate Style. We have also hosted over forty ATL Originals Skate Parties here in the ATL to keep Atlanta Skating alive. Atlanta has over fourteen different skating rinks and that's what sets us apart from any other state.

Now that we are in 2021, Kojak and I have decided to produce a documentary on our Atlanta Skate Culture. We are known as the OGs of ATLANTA SKATING.

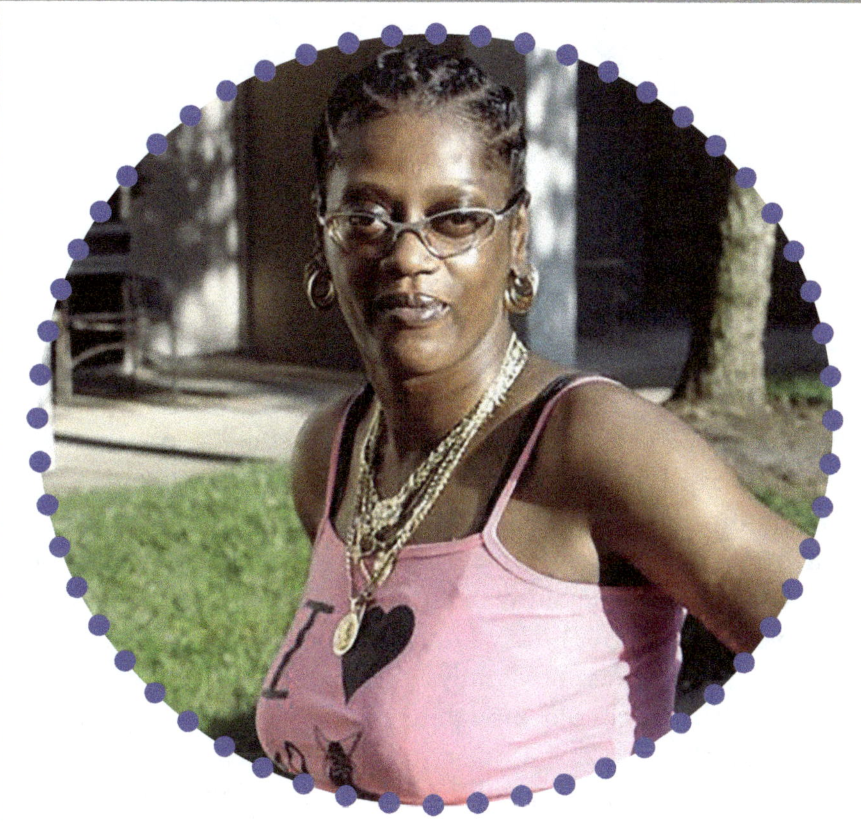

Sharon Lee

aka The Bus Queen

In January 2022, the skate community mourned the loss of an angel. Sharon left an indelible mark on the community. She is sorely missed.

"The Ride of Your Life"

I first fell in love with roller skating fifty-three years ago in my hometown of Newark, New Jersey. I used to watch people skating around in tutus, although back then, it was predominantly white people who had the run of the rinks. Neither of my parents skated; my mother had polio from the time of my birth, and my father passed away when I was seven years old. Whitney Houston's mother took me to the rink for the first time because her family and mine were close friends. When others on my block got old enough to go on their own, we began to go more frequently.

My first pair of skates were the clip-on skates with the key, but I only wore them for show; I didn't want anyone to see me in those skates. Instead, I wore the same pair of rental skates every time I went to the rink. I put a mark on them so I knew which ones were 'mine' because breaking in new rentals each week wasn't a good look. When I was able to get my first real pair of skates in 1973, I purchased a pair of Riedell boots with the Douglas Snyder plates, which were the best boots ever. I still have them, and they still look new. The new boots they make today are more for show and tell.

Known as the Bus Queen, I've been skating for fifty-three years. Thirty-five years ago, I started organizing bus routes. I began arranging these rides as I celebrate twenty-eight years of being clean and sober this year. People often like to let loose on skate trips, but I've always been the responsible one! My motto is simple: "Leave the driving to someone else so you can get to your destination safely!" If you plan to smoke or drink, I never encourage anyone to drive. That's why I initiated these bus trips—to ensure everyone's safety. The route typically took

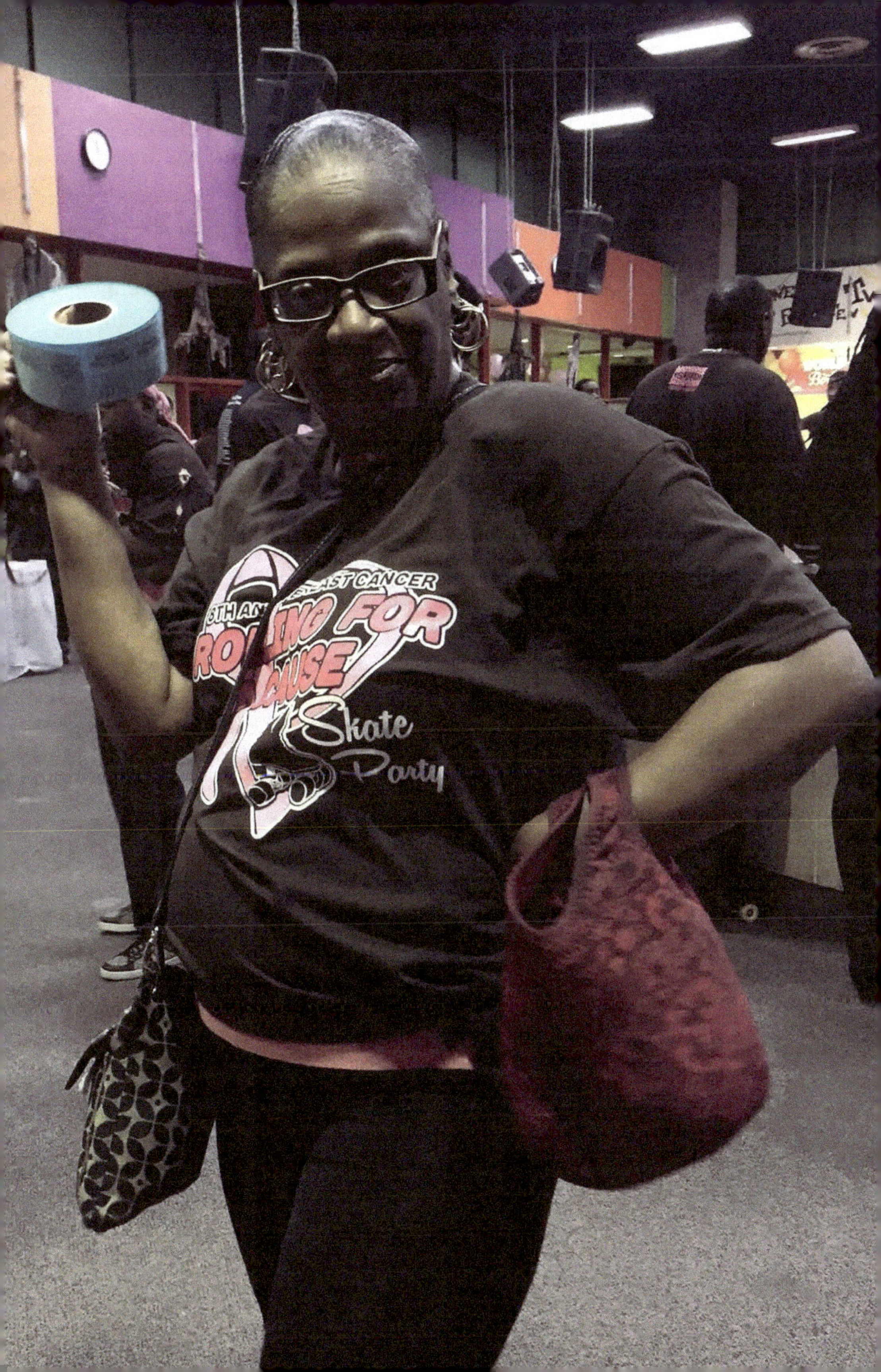
CANCER
FOR
Skate
Party

us into New York to pick up passengers before heading south to our skating destination. I truly enjoyed organizing these trips, although I'm unable to do so currently. Nonetheless, the people who used to travel with me always appreciated it. Some other groups have reached out and asked for assistance in coordinating trips, and I'm always willing to help. I've always been fair and ready to offer advice to those venturing out on their own. Usually, I'd have around forty-five people on the bus trips, which was a good number. While I rarely made money from these trips—safety, not profit, was always my priority—I must admit that most of the time, I ended up taking a significant loss. However, sometimes you have to take a loss to pursue the things you love; you can't always come out on top.

The most challenging aspect of organizing the bus rides was securing enough passengers. Typically, you have to pay the bus companies in advance, and if you don't get enough people to cover the trip, guess who loses out? I've also encountered unscrupulous individuals who took advantage of me. On one occasion, someone requested a bus ride for a skate trip but never paid after I covered the cost. I lost $1,500 and never received any restitution. It was a tough lesson, but I've never made that mistake again. It also took me a while to let go and let God with that individual due to their lack of integrity.

When someone took one of my bus rides, they knew that their entry fee for the rink was combined with their fare. Upon arrival at the venue, they never had to stand in line. The party host was always aware of our arrival, and it was as if we had VIP status! The host would open a side door or have an advance ticket line, so our party could enter the venue seamlessly. We enjoyed good food, cold drinks, and an even better time.

I had an excellent relationship with the rink owners and event coordinators. Once, when I fell ill and forgot the tickets at home, we still arrived at the venue. I called in advance and explained the situation to the organizer, who simply said, "Don't worry about it, Bus Queen!" They let all of my bus riders in without any issues. After composing myself, I went into the venue, thanked them, and skated for the last hour, shaking off whatever illness I had.

I only had two bad experiences with the bus trips. On one trip, some homeless people broke into the bus parked at the rink, and the skaters confronted them. The rink owner called me to come get my people, and when I asked why, he explained the situation. I told him those thieves had no business stealing from us. Man, those skaters went to work on them—men and women alike! The next time the bus pulled up to that rink, those homeless people were nowhere to be found.

The second incident involved a disagreement with my friend, resulting in a physical altercation where I accidentally kicked out the bus's back window. Despite offering to pay for the damage, the bus driver told me not to worry about it, as he had witnessed the entire incident. I had to stand up the entire ride home with a blanket over the broken window, but not a single shard flew in thanks to the precautions we took.

There was a time when a rented bus broke down, so we all got off the bus with our blankets and radios and set up an impromptu picnic on the side of the road. Everyone made the best of the situation, and although I was upset and started crying, the skaters comforted me, reminding me that stuff happens. All thirty of us sat there and enjoyed the great outdoors until another bus came to pick us up.

A few memories from organizing these bus rides still resonate with me today. Over twenty years ago, we took a bus trip to the Tristate, where the Tristate Divas prayed with us and prayed for our safe return home before we left their rink. Another memory was when another skate group filled our coolers with water and Gatorade for our trip back home. Little acts of kindness like these matter deeply, and the warmth in those gestures has stayed with me. The good experiences truly outweighed the bad when it came to these bus rides.In August 2008, I broke my back on a skate trip. There was no speeding or alcohol involved; the car I was riding in lost control due to hydroplaning in the rain. Since then, I've been unable to skate. Currently, I'm in a lot of pain, and even simple movements require rest afterward. Although I've tried to skate a few times since my injury, it hasn't worked out in my favor. I'm bedbound until we figure out exactly what's wrong, but don't worry—I've got one more run in me, and I'm coming back out! However, skating isn't the same as it used to be. I'm not going to risk getting back on the floor only to be knocked down and break bones because at my age, we don't heal as fast.

I've skated nationwide in places like Ohio, Atlanta, North Carolina, Virginia, St. Louis, Las Vegas, New York, New Jersey, and even Canada. I've never competed in any competitions; my style of skating is fast and outdoors. I'm a rider, and I can keep up with the best of them. I was in a skate group with a gentleman I dated back in the day called Tugger Productions. When he came out to skate, he took on the nickname Tugger, and together with a few others, we formed a small group. Our group won two Adrenalin Awards, and I have trophies from the manager, Gary, at Elmswhere Skating Rink—one for most represented and one for trains and trios. While some people claimed to be part of Tugger Productions, I'm not sure if I can say we were an official group. The crew consisted of Tugger and me, along with a young lady who cooked our food and another who designed our website.

We organized the First Thursdays at Branch Brook Park, which were some of the best skating events ever. While someone else had done it before us, our First Thursday Skate surpassed all expectations. We had a different DJ every Thursday, and we'd pull in a crowd of one thousand to fifteen hundred people each week from all over. We catered to our guests, providing food, ice-cold water, and raffling prizes like a color TV every week. I never skated on First Thursdays because as the host, I needed to be available for our guests. I'd meet and greet them, ensuring everyone had what they needed.

If I had to choose the best skating party I've ever attended, it would be Branch Brook Park during our First Thursdays. The second would be the closing event my friend Steve and I organized on a Saturday at Empire. We went double overcapacity, and they had to shut it down because it was so packed. Funk Master Flex was in the house, and helicopters flew over the event. We could have gone to jail that night, but they would have had to catch me—that's when my legs were good! While Empire wasn't my home rink, I frequented it on Tuesdays; Twin Cities was my home rink. Wherever my feet go, I am home. Many rink owners showed me love, and I appreciated that. I was raised to treat people the way I want to be treated, which is why Ice and I get along so well. He has a great sense of humor, and we always have a good time together.

Ice from Philly is my buddy, and other than his sense of humor, he's loyal and always there for me. We can talk about anything, cry, and sit on the phone for hours. Knowing that we're there for each other is a bond that can never be broken. We're real with each other—always. He's like a brother to me; we can call each other no matter the time of day or night. When my mother passed away, Ice came to her funeral in the pouring rain. We met at Millennial Skating Rink, and I had to let my friend Steve know that Ice was my friend and would be around. I think that solidified our friendship. Ice and Steve became fast friends, and here's a funny story about Ice: we were at the Maryland House, and a few older white people were sitting on a bench. Ice and Steve put on helmets like special kids and did a show for them on skates. They didn't clutch their bags; they relaxed and enjoyed the show. Everyone had a good time—that's just Ice's typical mode of operation!

Some of the biggest changes I've seen in the skate culture from then to now is that it seems like a lot of people are selfish. Skating is no longer seen as an art but more as a show. For me, skating is a pleasure, and even if I never get to skate again, I can still enjoy watching people skate on YouTube. My advice to new skaters is to leave their cell phones in their lockers—not in their pockets because if you fall, your screen could crack and leave glass on the floor. Hold your head up when you skate, and don't be afraid to ask for help when you need it. New jacks should stay in the middle and leave the outside for fast skaters. Roller skating is a beautiful thing, and it will last forever.

Some of the people who inspired me were Ice from Philly, Terminator Tex (God Rest His Soul), Little Mike Johnson (God Rest His Soul), Bill Butler, Charles Edwards, Stanley, Brandon, OooSoo, Mahaujah, Sandy aka The Black Fox, and many others. Sandy was one of the divas on the skate floor; she was amazing on those eights. I used to tell her she was a Bad "B," but the truth was, I admired her skate style to the fullest. Skating goes beyond footwork; I watch the way a person holds their arms and moves their body. Skating is amazing and will last forever!

Do You Know...

That Roller Skating Burns Calories?

An average-sized man who weighs around 190 pounds can expect to burn about 10 calories each minute of roller skating, while an average-sized woman weighing 163 pounds can expect to burn about 9 calories per minute. The calorie-burning benefits of roller skating add up quickly; you can burn between 300 and 600 calories if you skate for a full hour.

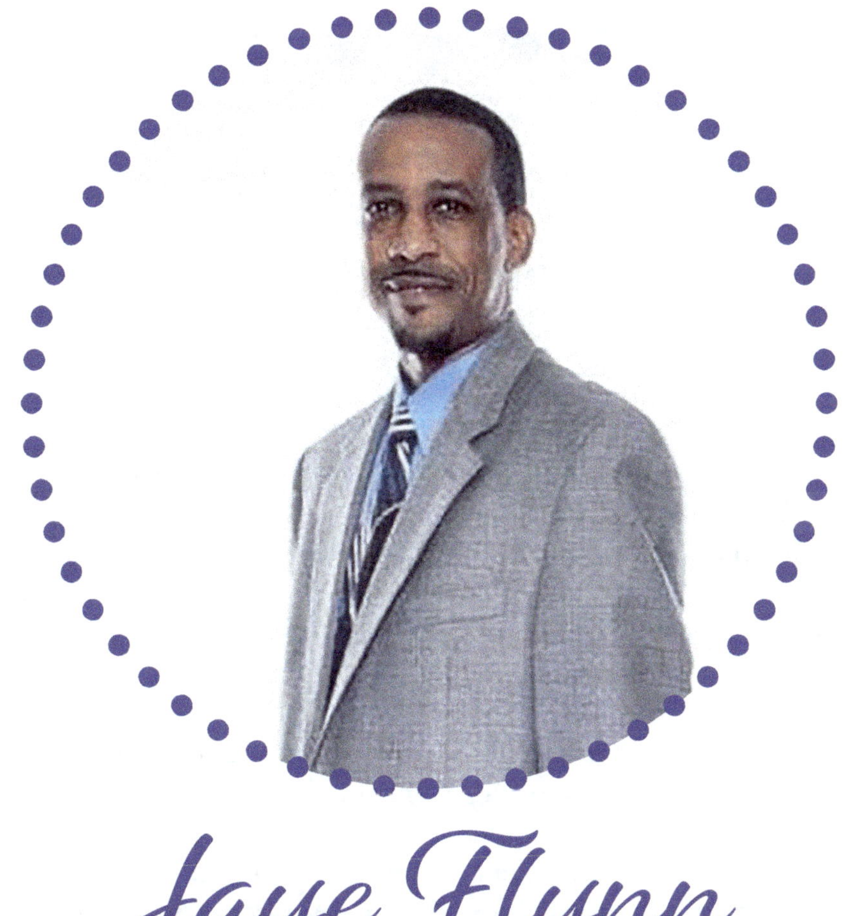

Jaye Flynn

aka The Cat With the Gold Plates

Facebook: @Jaye PThree Flynn | Instagram: bk.skydiver

"That Cat With the Gold Plates"

A journey that began a long time ago in a city far, far away... all started when four-year-old Jaye sneaked into his older sister's room at 7:00 a.m. on a Saturday—grabbing her metal skates. You know, the kind you slip your sneakers into and buckle with the leather ankle strap. I'd watched her put them on several times, so I figured, "I can do that!" So, I did, waddling and stumbling in the hallway of our Bushwick Brooklyn apartment.

Eventually, I got to shuffling my feet back and forth, not moving anywhere—but certainly making plenty of noise (metal wheels against parquet floors make for a very unique alarm clock). Needless to say, I got the fussing-out of the century for waking up the entire house—most notably by my mom. After a few more episodes of sneaking into my sister's skates, it was apparent to Mom that this is something I wanted to give a try. So, that next birthday, as fate would have it, I got a pair of 'strap-on' skates. Not the metal ones like my sister's, but the plastic ones (red and yellow Fisher-Price types).

I quickly burned through that pair, and a couple more after that. Until age nine, I got an upgrade with a pair of skates from Modell's Sporting Goods. They were black vinyl with yellow stripes and had a toe protector. You couldn't tell me nothing! From that moment, if you saw the young me, I had those skates on. In the grocery store with Mom, in the kitchen, up and down the hallway, in front of the apartment building—everywhere.

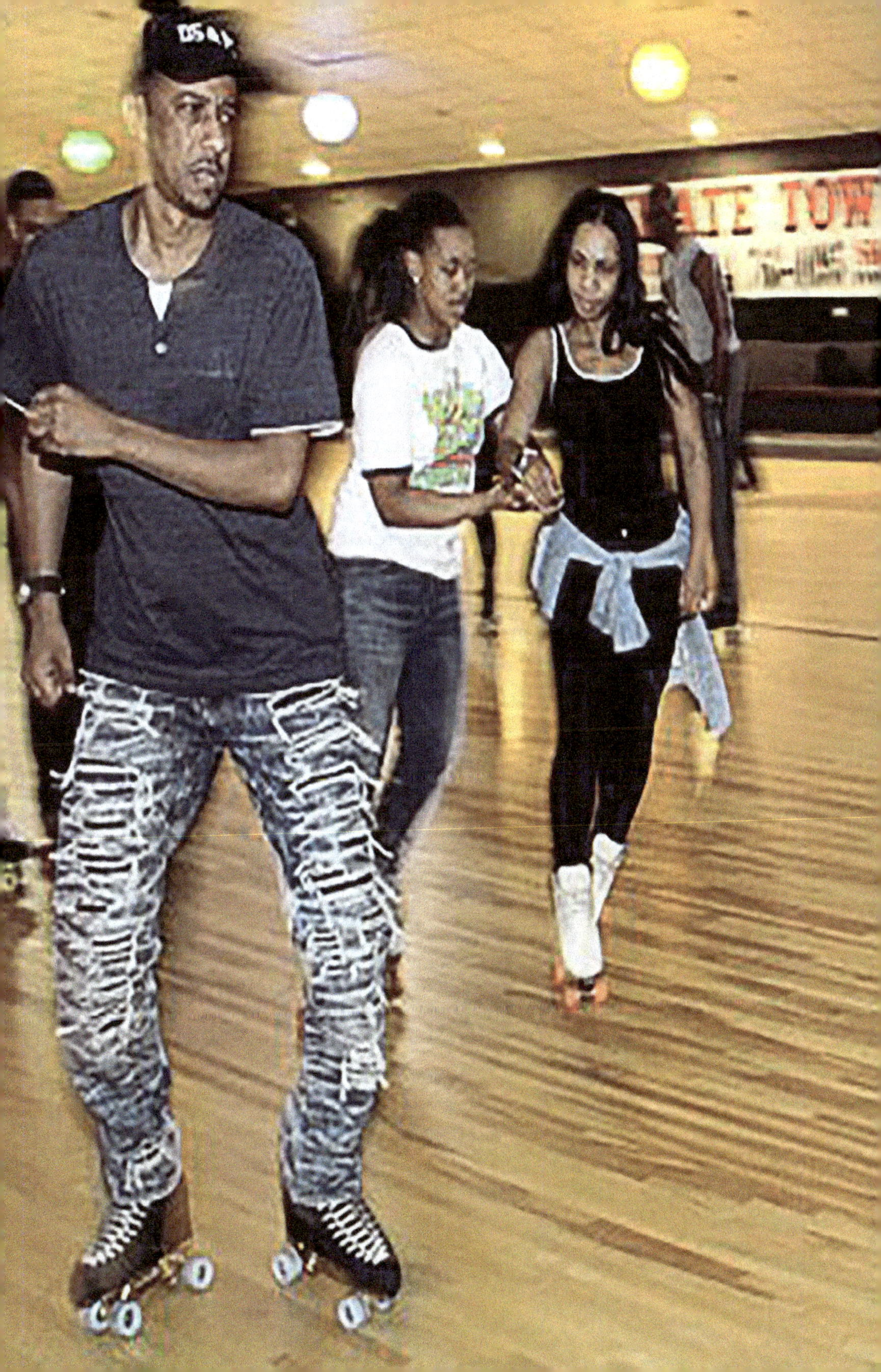

Yeah, it was clear from that moment, skating started a new chapter in my life. My family had recently moved into a new apartment complex in East New York—Starrett City. It wasn't a far move because, before that, I lived in the Cozine Ave apartments which were two blocks away. The move to Starrett City is important because it meant twenty-story high rises with multi-level parking garages and freshly paved streets which equated to absolute perfection in the mind of an inner-city skater. Most other kids I knew that didn't live in Starrett City wished they did because of the smooth streets as well as the brand-new basketball and handball courts. Another cool perk was that we could hold onto the back of city buses and they would pull us for nearly a mile down Van Siclen Ave, all the way to the entrance of the Belt Parkway (that's the equivalent of the highway for those not familiar with the area). We had the time of our lives playing Ringolevio and Round-up until the street lights came on.

Nearly all my free time went to doing some form of skating in the street. Skating in the street provided the foundation for nearly everything I do on skates to this day. Street skating taught me how to be light on my feet because, in the street, there are numerous hazards you don't often find at an indoor roller rink such as cracks in the concrete, pebbles, water puddles, and sharp elevation changes. I was about ten or eleven years old before I ever skated in an indoor rink. It was during a school trip to Roll-A-Palace in Sheepshead Bay in Brooklyn. I had an absolute blast and after that—it was all I could think about—indoor rinks, that is.

Mainly because I could skate regardless of the weather and the sound systems were better than my boom box in the park. I also remember attending a birthday party at Laces in Long Island and even bumped into Salt-n-Pepa in the middle. As I got older and a bit better at holding my own, I began hitting as many rinks as I could: Skate Key on Allerton Ave in the Bronx, The Roxy in lower Manhattan, The Rink in Bergenfield New Jersey; Skate 22 out in Union New Jersey, United Skates on Fordham Rd in the Bronx, United Skates in Jackson Heights.

Mind you, some of these rinks I had to either sneak into with a fake ID or go in with someone I knew who worked there, but no matter what—I was gettin' in! Taking two and three trains and a bus sometimes from Brooklyn where I lived to parts of New Jersey where there was no mass transit—it didn't even matter, it was about skating with different people who had different styles and flows. Back then it was about sharing your flow, getting better, learning something from the next cat and incorporating it into your flow, and making it your own.

I remember going on a school trip to a lesser-known rink in Bed Stuy. Despite its unassuming exterior, stepping inside completely transformed my world. Empire! Just mentioning its name in any skating circle evokes instant recognition worldwide. It's like the Michael Jordan, Lambeau Field, and Yankee Stadium of roller-skating rolled into one. Every skater knows someone who's been there, and that someone is held in high regard for good reason. While I'd been to indoor rinks before, Empire was different—it was alive, it had a soul. With three rinks— a large one comparable to Roll-A-Palace, a smaller one nestled within, and another separate rink at the rear—Empire was unparalleled. And the sound system? Unmatched, with speakers the size of sofas! Let's not forget the stage bridging the main rink and the smaller one, where both local and national singers and Hip-Hop artists performed and shot music videos. I was in awe. A classmate, knowing one of the floor guards, invited me back for a Saturday night session. Little did I know what awaited me. The energy was electric and unceasing. Unlike other rinks where sessions were punctuated with breaks, Empire kept the momentum going. It felt like hours of skating before the DJ signaled for specials. And when they did, it was unlike anything I'd experienced—reverse skate, among others, adding to the excitement. I left that night drenched in sweat, buzzing with energy. The entire train ride home, all I could think about was returning. But there was a hitch—I was only fourteen, and Empire's sessions were for those twenty-one and older. My focus shifted from saving for admission to saving to grease the floor guard's palm with $10. That's when my love affair with skating truly began.

Empire was certainly the place to be on Friday (18 and up) and Saturday nights (21 and up). On Fridays, it was 8 pm-1 am and you had to get there early at like 8:30 pm so you could get your smooth slow tempo music in before it got heavy. DJ Big Bob was a staple and sometimes Sting International would play. I have an old soul so I enjoyed Big Bob's style—he gave you that old school R&B and real Hip Hop and would sometimes sing and hum over the instrumentals and have you straight vibin! On any given night, he would even hit you with the reggae and dance hall and have the middle packed—some people skating, some people dancing and some just playing chess and enjoying the scene. But then on Saturday nights, it was sumthin' else'—it was 9:30 pm-3:30 am and lemme tell you, you had to take your vitamins and bring at least two to three extra t-shirts because whatever you had on when you came in would be soaking wet with sweat by the 1st hour—no question! There wasn't an adult session at any rink I knew that hit you with six hours of high-quality music like that!

After graduating high school and partway through college, I joined the Navy and became stationed in Norfolk, Virginia. This was certainly a different skating scene than I had known. I started out skating at College Park in Virginia Beach and I remember they had an actual house stereo as their sound system–crazy! Regardless, it was an experience and enabled me to meet some great friends there who introduced me to several other rinks in the area such as Plaza in Hampton, Main Street in Newport News, and the Rollerdome in Richmond, Virginia. I liked the floor at the Rollerdome as well as the music local radio DJ Kirby Carmichael played so, I began making the one-and-a-half-hour drive on Sunday nights to get my roll on. It was there that I met then twenty-year-old Mike 'Diddy' Giles. We became fast friends; so much so that people used to say if you saw me, you saw Diddy—some people even thought we were related.

Shortly after leaving the military, I settled in Northern Virginia. I would ride my sport bike out to Richmond to skate with Diddy at Rollerdome and sometimes at the Hull Street rink. This was a rather pivotal time for both Diddy and me because he was just starting to really formulate his skate style and organically, he began to incorporate my New York style of skating into his own. Shortly thereafter, he introduced me to his best friend Lawrence 'Jit' Thomas, and just like that, the three of us were inseparable at the rink. It wasn't long before Diddy started making the drive up to my house and we would ride together on Saturday nights to skate at Skateland in Towson, Maryland. They had an amazing floor, where Daniel JB Burton and KW Griff would DJ—and Daniel would pack the rink. He had a bread truck full of equipment and he would have the sound system thumpin!

The more Diddy and I skated together—the more in sync we got. So much so that we had a pretty decent following at the rinks we frequented—we would always tear the middle up! Freestylin', figure 8s, even 'battles' with some of the local skate groups. You couldn't tell us anything! We were sort of famous, or so we liked to think. Our notoriety became so well-known across Richmond, Petersburg, and Hampton Roads—skaters from all points began to emulate our skate style—the New York Style! Diddy and Jit began to teach their friends some of the pivots and turns. Eventually, our small group of three became a group of four (Sam Fonville). Virginia's skate landscape was forever changed—chiefly due to skaters sharing their love and passion for the craft!

I mentioned to Diddy that I was going to Brooklyn to visit family and before I could finish my sentence, he said, "I wanna go!" So out of respect, I assured 'Momma Giles' that I would take good care of her son the entire time we were away. We stayed at the Marriott by the Brooklyn Bridge and we shopped like tomorrow wasn't coming! I made sure we ate good and got back to the hotel in time to rest because I knew something that Diddy didn't—Big Bob was DJing that night and Empire was gonna wear both of us out—yeah, I said it! That night, Bob was in his bag and Diddy got to see some of the skate legends that made me the skater I am—Mike Johnson (RIP), Lawrence 'Skates' Smith, Eric Alston, Kurby Brown, Randy White, Starrah Gilmore-Jones, Katina 'KatSkates' Cadlett, Lauretta Lawrence and so many more. He was now able to connect the dots to understand some of the roots behind the pivots, the turns, the hand jive, and edge control that he learned from me. This is how skate skills evolve and transform into a flow. This is what skating means to me.

After a few years living in Northern Virginia, I moved back to Brooklyn for a job opportunity. As you can imagine I was taking full advantage of being able to skate at my home rinks again. I hit Empire on Tuesdays, Skate 22 in New Jersey on Wednesdays, Branchbrook on First Thursdays, and when I wanted to work on my edges I would even skate with the 18 and up crowd on Fridays back at Empire (the kid sessions will make your work). As fate would have it, while at Empire one Tuesday night I met one of the most pivotal individuals I would encounter throughout my skating journey—Michele McPhun. She was handing out flyers advertising a 15-passenger van trip to The Rink in New Jersey. Michele marketed the trip as a cost-saving way for us to skate without the burden of each person having to drive and pay tolls. Genius, huh? Well back then it truly was a genius move. So, I bought my ticket, rode the van, skated and had a great time, and slept the whole ride back. Michele coordinated several more of these trips—some to rinks in New Jersey, some to rinks in other states like Skateland in Towson, Maryland. These trips grew in popularity such that a 15-passenger van was no longer enough—she began to rent motor coaches to fill the demand. Little did we know it then, but this was the start of what we now call "skate parties." This quickly evolved into tri-state, regional, and eventually international events. These skate parties connected skaters from all over the world and enabled an organic fellowship where new friendships form—ones that can last a lifetime. This is the impact skating has had on my life.

Fun fact—most skaters observe me skating and remark that I have great balance—that couldn't be further from the truth. My balance is horrible; skating just masks it very well. A quote I stand by—we are born and then we die. The difference is in the intensity with which we live. I have seen countless friends and family nearing the end of their lives and one common thread they each shared is having regrets about things they wish they would have done. So, to all who read this I say, Live life abundantly!

The following are just a handful of the most influential people who have had a notable impact in shaping my skate journey. I am eternally grateful to each of them, as well as those not mentioned, who, whether or not they know it, are part of me and everything I left on the wood; Sandy "Black Fox" Bryson, Nicole "KatSkates" Cadlett, Starrah Gilmore-Jones, Eric Alston, Sandy Bryson, Hayden Williams, Jessica "The Jess" Andrew, Joana "Jo' Bulmer, Gloria "GloBug" Downs, and Brian "Killa B" Taylor.

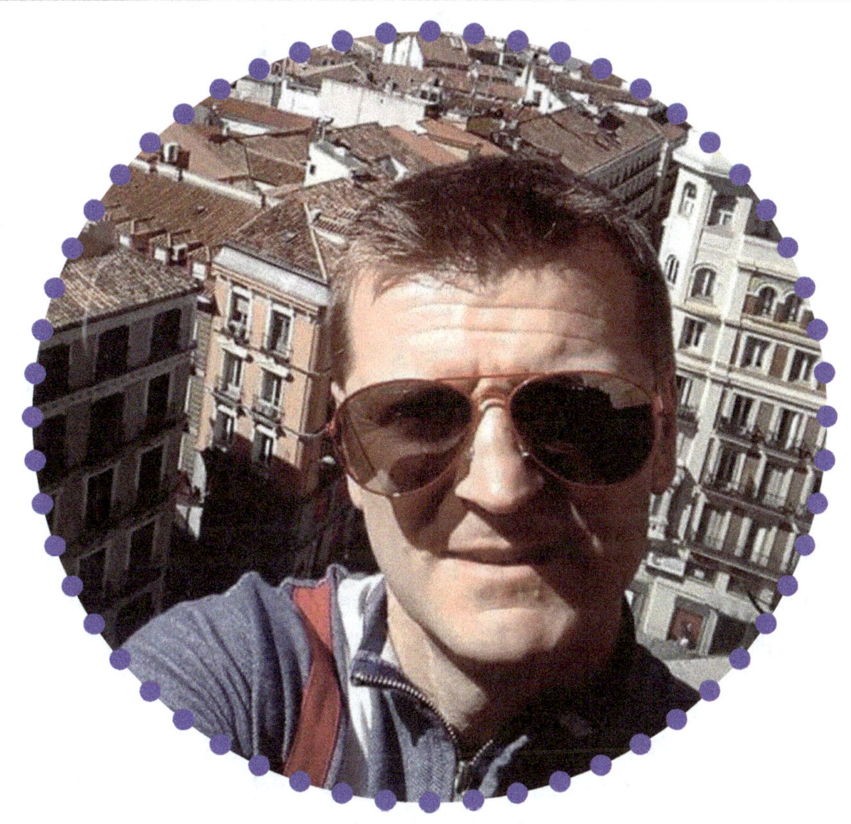

Kris Ward

aka Skatemeister

Facebook: @Kris Skatemeister Ward | Instagram: @skate_meister

"The UK and Beyond"

My story began when I was between fifteen and sixteen years old, back in 1984, during my time at school when I decided to give ice hockey a try. While I wasn't a very skilled player, I could skate decently and found joy in it. Playing ice hockey for Brighton in the United Kingdom (UK) for four years led me to participate in four tournaments in Holland. I thoroughly enjoyed every aspect of the competition and had fun doing what I loved. During that period, I was heavily involved in music and embarked on a career as a DJ for another four years.

After a fifteen-year hiatus from skating, I decided to attend the London Street Skate in 2010. This event inspired me to organize a street skate of our own in Brighton. Serendipitously, while skating along the Brighton seafront, I met Liam Boraman, with whom I shared my idea of starting our local street skate.

Being born and raised in Brighton, I was familiar with the area. Taking action, I printed paper flyers to promote our inaugural street skate. Twelve skaters showed up at our very first event. Since London Skate featured music, we aimed to match—if not surpass—their setup. I customized my old DeWalt radio and revamped a backpack to amplify the sound. Initially, this setup worked well, and as our skate grew, so did our sound system. Skaters contributed donations to enhance our audio equipment. Collaborating with various skaters, we built a lightweight, radio-linked sound system to take our roller disco to the streets and spread the vibes. My friend Stuart Holt possessed exceptional technical skills; he could construct and modify any sound system, and he supported us throughout the years. Now, twelve years later, we have over seventeen hundred members, with four of us remaining from the inaugural year—what a journey it has been!

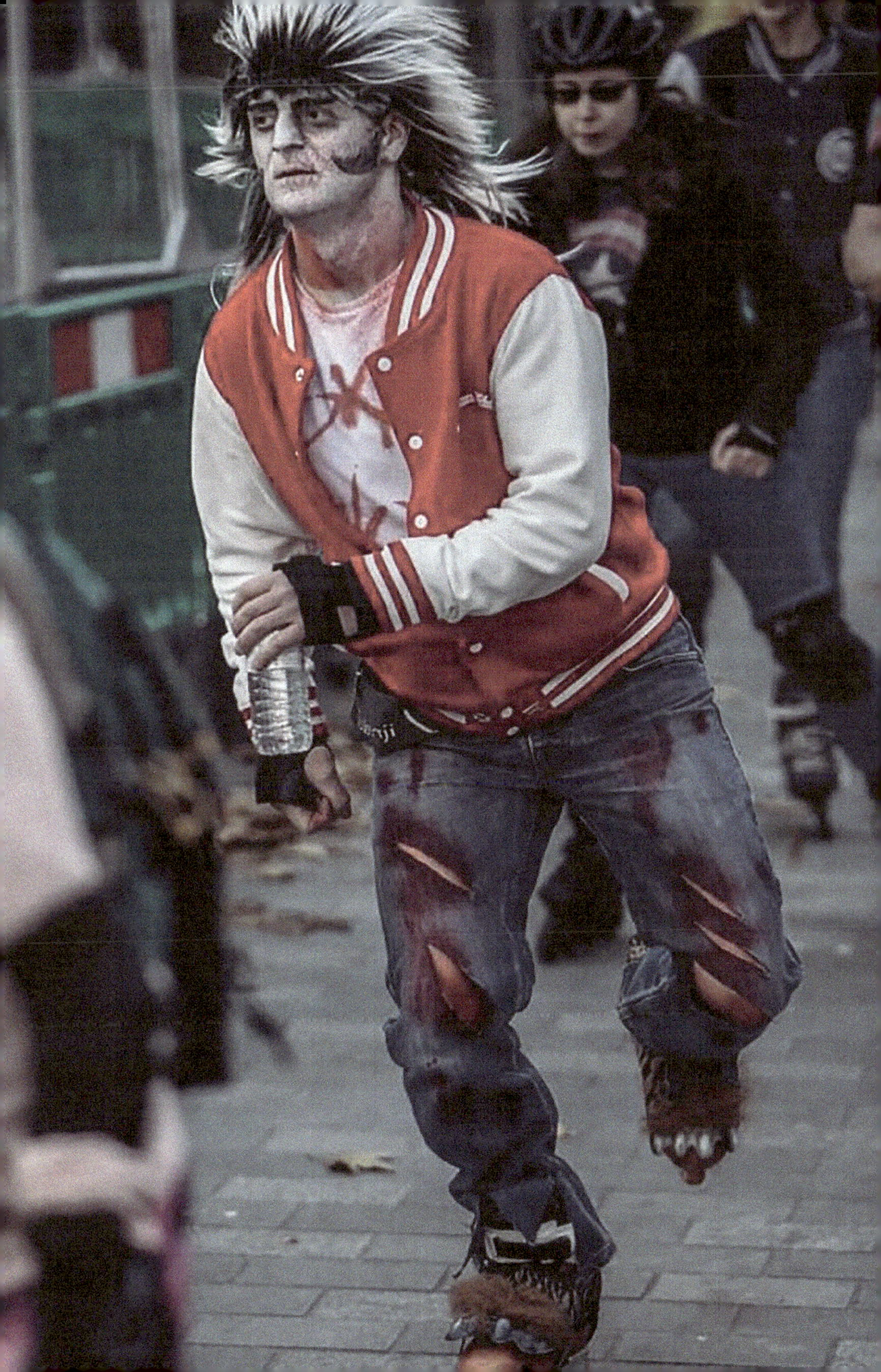

Our first skate trip took us to Madrid, Spain, which sparked the convergence of three Spanish skate groups— all for our benefit! Following that night, the Madrid Friday Night Skate (MFNS) was established. The skate grew to the extent that it required a police escort. We revisited Madrid four times to explore the incredible routes throughout the city, including a nine-mile gentle downhill. After my last trip to Madrid, we received an invitation to Rolling Dance and Burger, a roller disco that exceeded my expectations. Following that skate session, dance fever swept through the scene, igniting my desire to learn more. We ventured to Sevilla, Spain, where we skated on the set of Star Wars—an exhilarating experience for a Star Wars enthusiast like myself. Subsequently, we learned about SKATE LOVE BARCELONA. Naturally, a group of Brighton skaters attended the event, alongside skaters from across the UK, Europe, and the USA. Needless to say, we all had an amazing time!

Back in the UK, we decided to host our skate dance event in a unique outdoor space by the seafront, beneath a cliff face. By shining a torch on the cliff face, we created a thirty-foot high silhouette of the skaters against the cliff.

Despite the pandemic in 2020, I had some incredible moments with great friends in the UK, Europe, and the USA. I also participated in ZOOM sessions with DJ ARSON throughout the year (Make Room in That Zoom). In Brighton, where we lack a roller rink and rely mainly on sports halls, skating outside is largely dependent on the weather—especially during the pandemic.

One day, I hope to skate in Central Park NYC, Venice Beach, and Golden Gate Park, if the Skate Gods permit. My journey in the skate world has been truly remarkable thus far, and I want to extend my heartfelt thanks to all those who have been on this journey with me.

Skating isn't about how skilled you are, but rather, how much you love to skate. Now, lace up your skates and hit the streets.

Special thanks to: Simon Pert (sound bike), Asha Kirkby (SKATEFRESH.COM), Stuart Holt (audio technician), Stuart Grace (videographer), Jim Morrow AKA Jimmy Blaze, Hjalti Halldorsson (audio technician), Jake Eley (Locoskates.com). Many thanks to the Marshalls and everyone else who has contributed to the skate community.

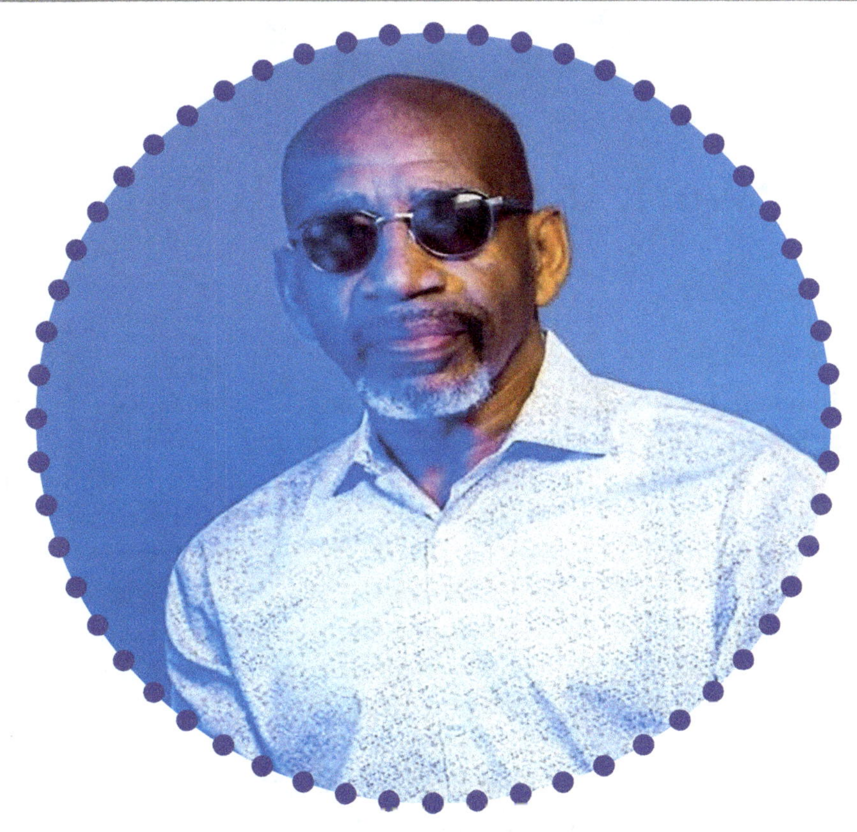

Jay Burno

aka Master Jay

Instagram: @masterjay52

"Work it Out, Work it Out"

I did not always roller skate. My life started a little bit slow in my love for roller skating. I grew up in Philadelphia and started skating as a kid. Growing up I did not skate often. I went skating with my family about once or twice a month. We went to Carman Roller Skating Rink, located in North Philly. As a teenager, I started traveling and visited Cincinnati, Ohio. I had my first roller skating experience here, and it was fantastic. I could see and feel how everyone in this skating arena connected through skating. This experience is what made me what to be a part of the roller-skating scene.

While visiting Cincinnati, I met a girl who was good at roller skating. She came to visit me in Philadelphia. She wanted to skate all the time. This is how I started roller skating more. I started being and feeling connected. Later, I started skating with friends in Philadelphia. That's when I met Sir Vince and a girl named Jerry. One day while out skating, someone approached us. They offered $150 to skate on the sidewalk outside of a store for three hours. This was my first roller skating gig. After that gig, we called our trio, 'Rhythm on Wheels.' This is where skating shifted from being a hobby to something I could make money doing. Later, we recruited more skaters to perform with us. Our group was an eclectic and diverse group of people from all different races and walks of life. At a point, there were eleven of us performing together, and it was beautiful. As a group, we skated at various events including private parties, roller skating venues, school assemblies, and parades around town.

Roller skating at Penn's Landing was monumental to my career in entertainment. I loved hanging out and skating outside every Saturday and Sunday there from 12 PM to 7 PM. My crew and I usually skated in

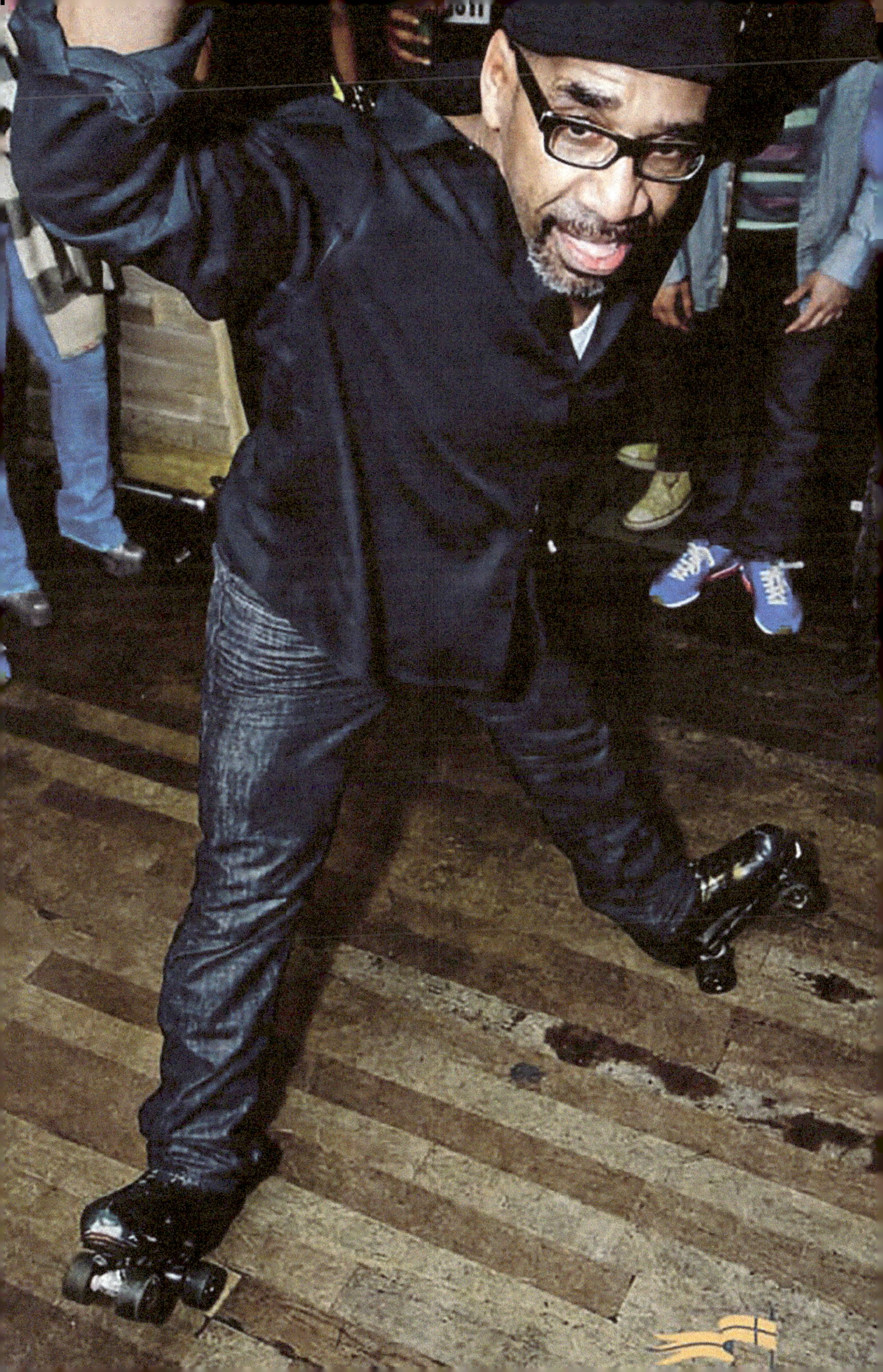

front of three tall buildings called Society Hill Towers. Penn's Landing was so euphoric for my crew and me because skating there became a routine thing for us. After some time, skaters would come and join us; people would bring their kids out to skate. Crowds of 30 to 150 people would crowd Penn's Landing watching us perform and have a wonderful time. We never took money while we were performing because it was for the love of skating we were out there. Penn's Landing became our second home and practice arena. We loved meeting and connecting with new people. Street performing and socializing with different people prepared me for the life as a professional skater. Roller skating at Penn's Landing was the start of my touring and entertainment career.

While skating at Penn's Landing I met a girl that danced with Waves Dance Company of Philadelphia. I skated into the studio looking to meet her. Instead, I received an invitation to do a small demo for the dance troop. After seeing my skate demo, they hired me on the spot and asked me to be a part of the crew. They were preparing for a tour at the time and asked me to join. I performed as the only roller skate dancer with the jazz dance company for over fifteen years. I continued to tour with Rhythm on Wheels until the crew dissolved, and we went our separate ways. Over that span of fifteen years, I toured in sixteen cities across the United States. I skated in California, New York, Atlantic City, and Chicago. Also in Oregon, Seattle, Delaware, and Wisconsin. I had the opportunity of touring internationally in countries like England (London), France (Paris), and Poland.

Roller skating has been a great part of my life for the last thirty-five years. It's been a blessing to have earned money while skating. I've met tons of beautiful people and had loads of experiences that were phenomenal. Skating is still an essential part of my life, and I continue to skate to this day. I enjoy a great deal watching the rise of the new generation of skaters coming through. I am honored to still be able to skate with them. I had the opportunity to assist my daughter's roller dance crew, 'Great on Skates' in Philadelphia. She administers beginner to advanced classes that I can have a hand in helping teach when I can. I teach the skate students roller dance routines that my crew and I loved doing. I still love doing these routines. Moves that made me fall into roller skating and extending to the new generation. Skating has been a blessing to me, I am over sixty and it blesses me to still be skating.

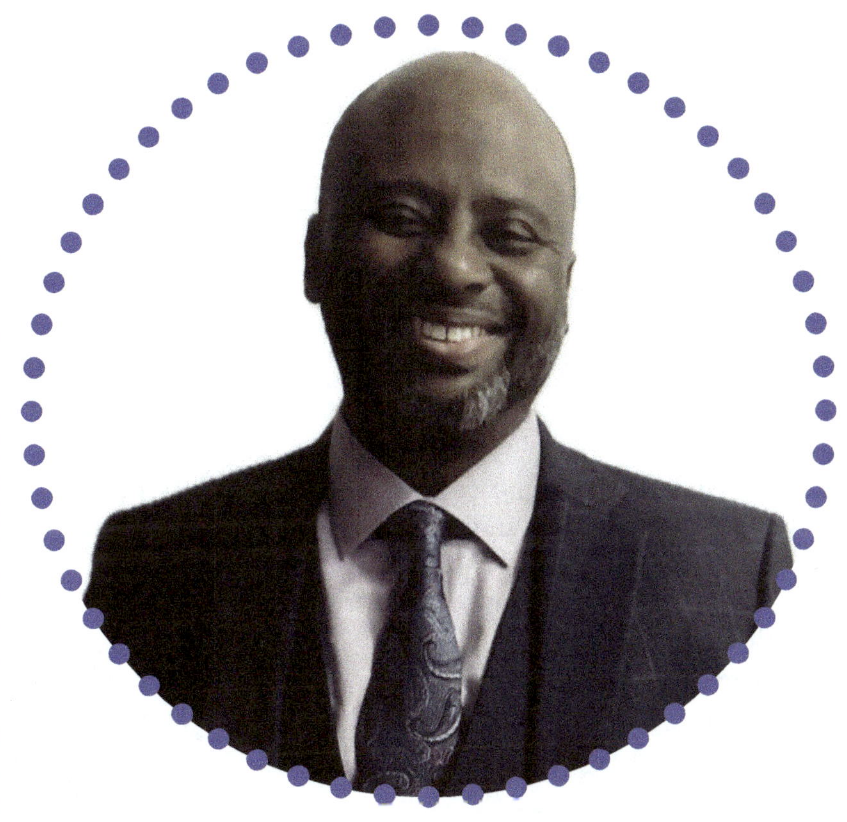

Kenneth Perdue

aka Crash Dummy

Facebook:FB: Kenneth L. Perdue
Instagram: @RollingBuckeyez Foundation

"Rollin Buckeyez"

I used to love skating until I turned it into a business. Or maybe it was all those matching headbands that rubbed out my hairline. Now, I have to wear hats all the time to hide my big forehead. And then there was the nickname, Crash Dummy, that stuck with me for every failed stunt I tried on skates!

It was 1978, I was sitting in the back seat of a Fleetwood with my cousins, heading to the Old Palace in Golden Gate to watch people in tight shorts and big afros skate. I had never seen so many happy and beautiful faces. I knew then that I wanted to be there. When I got home, I asked for fireball skates or a pair with metal wheel straps. Although my mom was a good skater from the Blue Goose, I could never get a pair. There were too many of us and not enough money. I would sneak off to the Salvation Army on 58th. It had a rink in the basement, but I wasn't there to skate; I was there to admire those pretty faces and tight shorts! It wouldn't be until ten years later that I would be fully committed and wouldn't miss a beat.

As far back as I can remember, our city has had plenty of roller rinks. Over the years, I've seen them come and go. Some have stayed, while others are at risk of disappearing. I've enjoyed many of them all around the country, traveling state-to-state with my family. Experiencing different styles and music, meeting new friends—this has only deepened my love and respect for the culture. These travels even led me to meet my beautiful wife, Dana, who loves roller skating even more than I do! It's one of the reasons our marriage has lasted over eighteen years! We have three children, Diamond, Jalen, and Jabari, who

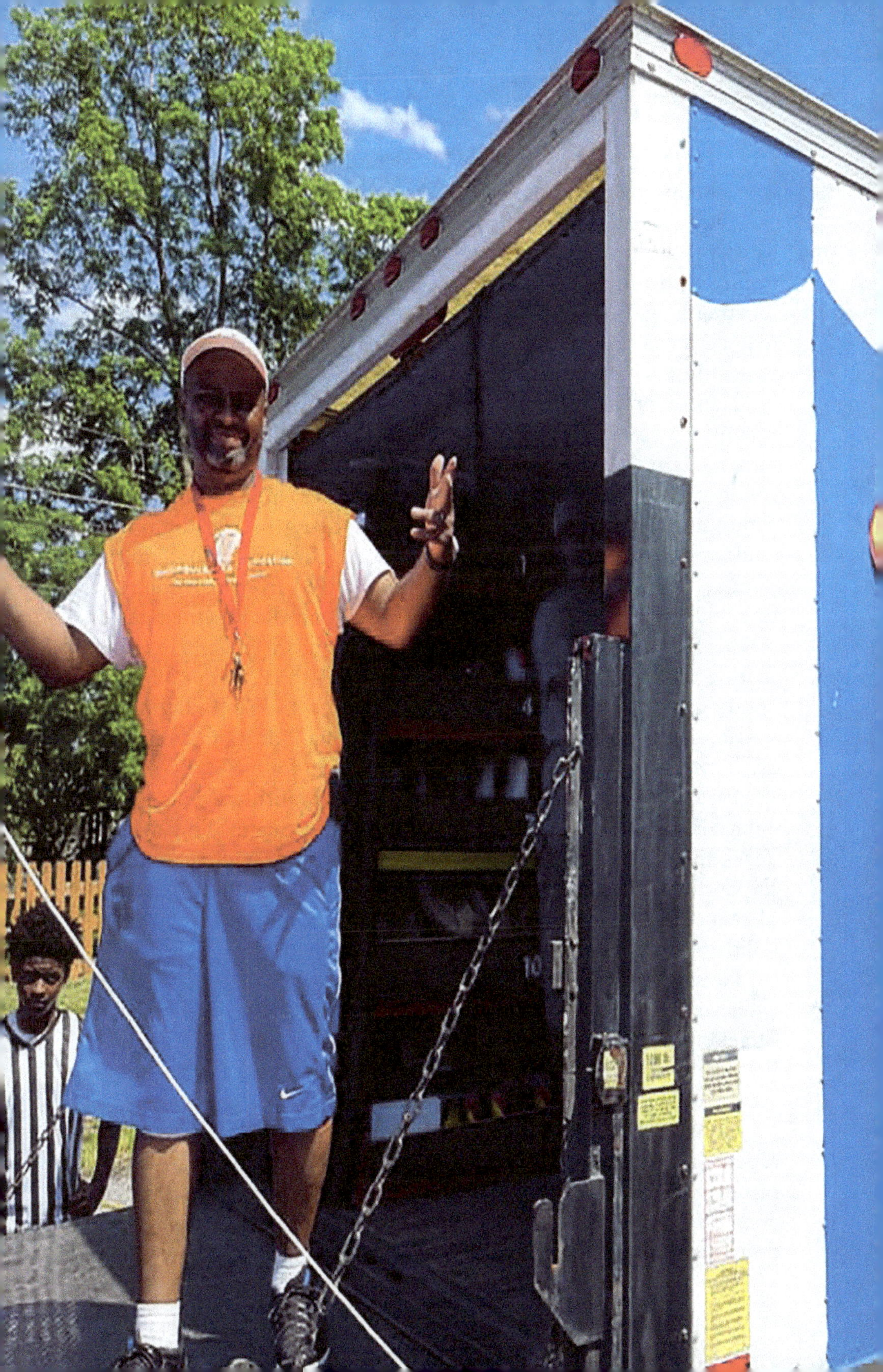

love to skate, and Lil Kenney, who isn't quite there yet. Roller skating is our happy place, and no one can take that away from me ever again!

Family and friends often say, "Ken, you're the glue. We need you." I know that I'm the person the community looks up to. I didn't set out to prove it to myself, but for everyone. My calling is to bring families together in an intergenerational, diverse social environment. Listening to good music and enjoying the ambiance of our city is what I envision. It was time for me to create something lasting.

I am a product of inner-city Cleveland, Ohio, off 71st in the Historical Hough Community to be exact. Without my paternal father in my life, I understand the importance of programming in young people's lives. After running away to escape the impoverished community that embraced me as a child, being part of the program while still living in the community molded me into the man I am today.

I set out to create a program that evolved from my hobby, so I founded Rink-in-the-Box a Pop-up rink. I am the executive director of the RollinBuckeyez Foundation, a nonprofit that brings roller skating to communities while promoting healthy lifestyles and family bonding. Conveniently located near the Rock and Roll Hall of Fame in Cleveland, Ohio, as we grew, we noticed that kids wanted more from us. They would say, "What are you going to do for us?"

Perdue's event calendar expanded with monthly events and live entertainment. Some events, like the Greatest Skate Show and New Year's Eve lock-ins, were big hits. We also hosted small get-togethers. Expanding to food drives, giving away hundreds of book bags full of school supplies, along with "Skating Santa" toy drives around the holidays, rounded out our efforts.

Now, evolving as a nonprofit, RollinBuckeyez brings our H.E.A.L. (Health, Exercise, Arts, Literacy) curriculum to parks and Pop-up Street events all over the city. Providing hundreds of local children their first-ever pair of roller skates has allowed thousands the opportunity to embrace the groove at a park or nearby event.

My life is so much more than this bio. Roller skating is just one aspect of my life that I am honored to share. To be part of history, to inspire generations to come—this is priceless. I've been part of so much good and so much controversy. Those who take issue with controversy don't matter, and those who matter don't mind. Through my passion and hobby, I've created a legacy. I hope to inspire many generations to come. I'm thankful for the community that I ran from, which then opened its arms to me and gifted a building to our organization. They believed in me—on the same corner where I grew up. Funny how the universe works!

Do You Know...

That Roller Skating is Good For Your Heart?

The American Heart Association recognizes roller skating as an effective aerobic exercise that helps strengthen the heart. According to research conducted at the University of Konstantz, moderate roller skating increases a skater's heart rate to levels ranging from 140 to 160 beats per minute, while skating at top speeds can increase heart rate up to around 180 beats per minute.

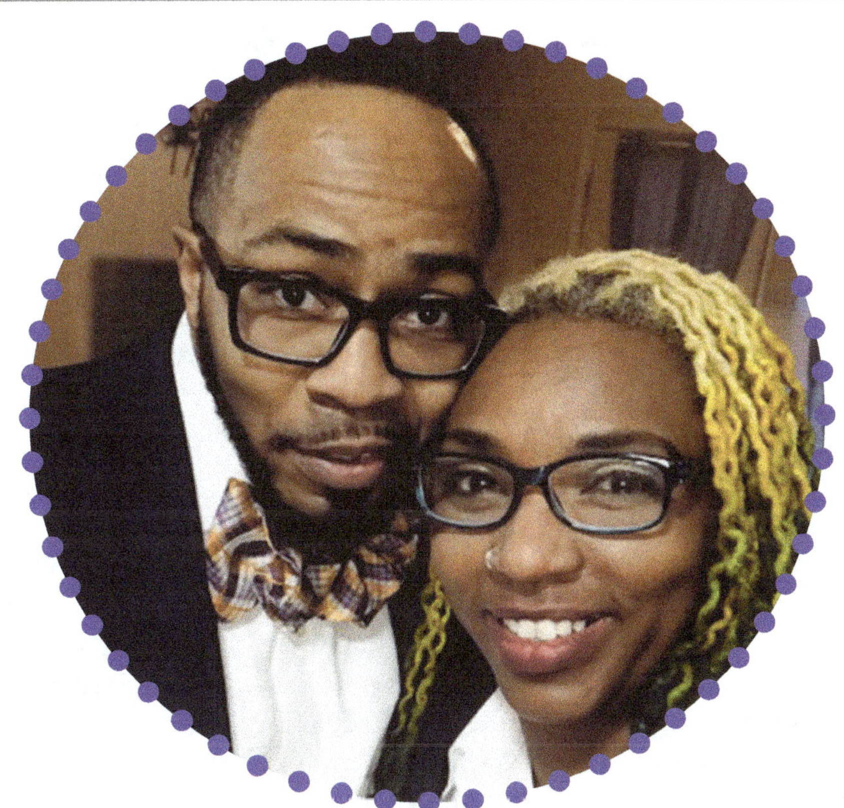

Demitrius & Denise Knowles

aka Dee and 1 Country Cutie

Facebook: @Denise Edmonson-Knowles | @Demitrius Knowles
Instagram: @mrs_d_knowles | @dee1dj2

"Meet on the Wood, Roll Until..."

Every Sunday, my god-sister Meme and I would hit the skating rink and roll as if our lives depended on it. Anytime we could roll, we would just do that. Then, one day, she invited me to attend something she called 'National Skate Parties.' As a kid, I saw skaters on the beach, but it was only when I watched CHIPS on TV. I never imagined people from different cities, all over the world, could love skating the same as me. Skate clubs, skate styles, skate DJs. It was a dream come true, and I immediately started traveling all over the country to skate.

One of the greatest gifts of the skate world is all the wonderful people you meet. The friendships that have opened through the years continue to grow. The love is indescribable. One skate party that sticks out in my mind is the Dogg Pound Skate Crew's MLK weekend in Huntsville, Alabama, in 2014. At that time, I was a single mother of three, divorced, and happy with myself and my life. My children and I were good. For the first time in a long time, I was at peace and was having some fun for myself. I had no idea the universe was brewing something that could only be from God.

The Dogg Pound Karaoke contest was one of the funniest events of the weekend. I'd met a group of people from Arkansas who right away became family. There was this crazy guy who looked young with them. His name was Dee (short for Demitrius) from Memphis. He skated with the Rolling Wheels of Memphis and was funny. Mr. CRAZY FOR NO DAMN REASON funny. Early on, we claimed we were

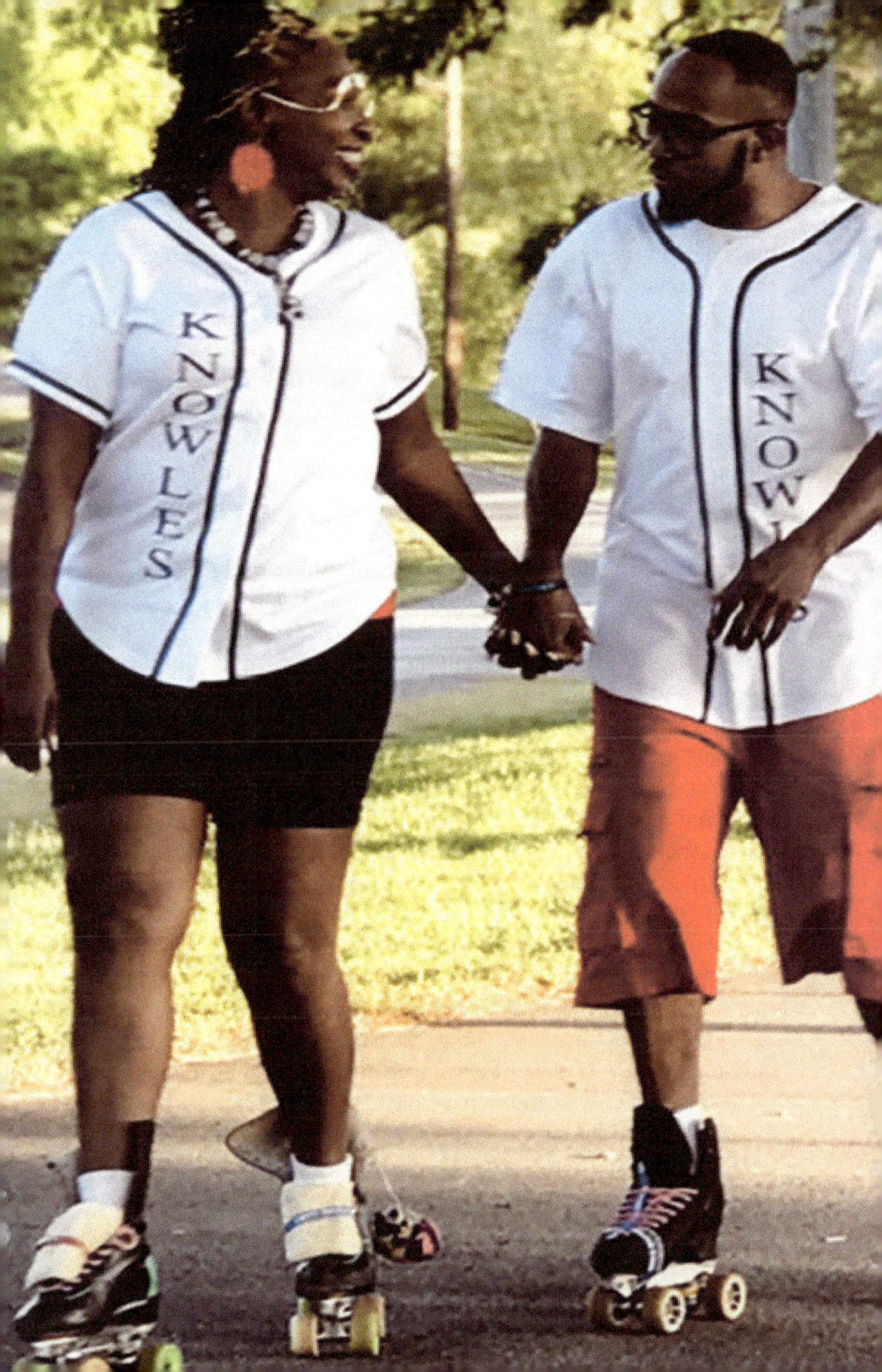
KNOWLES

"kicking it," but he was my boyfriend from the first time he called me two weeks after we met.

Dee and I did not see one another for a month after that first meeting, but we made up for it on the phone. It was like a flashback to our teenage years.

After a few weeks, he asked me out for our first 'official' date. It was a Valentine's Day skate party hosted by the Rolling Wheels of Memphis. What could be a better first date—roller skating and Valentine's Day? That was the first of many weekends we shared. Every weekend with one another, we managed to skate somewhere different. He put a ring on it not long thereafter. We've been wildly in love ever since! Despite the challenges we have faced, of which there have been plenty. Had God not played conductor between us, when I saw him rolling around at the skate jam, we wouldn't have become who we are today—as individuals, and as one.

My mother introduced roller skating to me when I was three years old. She was looking for something for me to do, and I immediately loved it, and I love it as much to this very day. Some people think it's a hobby, but it's more than that. Rolling is essential to my being. I can skate alone, and I can skate with friends. I can skate with my lover, Dee, who still invites me out on dates to this very day.

Some people don't get it. When I tell them about traveling to skate parties, they say, "Why would you do all that driving to skate when we have a rink right here?"

When you enjoy doing something, you expose yourself to that something on a higher level, why wouldn't you love it? Seems simple enough to me, yet, when I invite someone to a skate party, and they say that it feels like a slap to the face.

Skate parties opened me up to traveling like nothing else before—not only for me but for my kids as well. Receiving an invitation to that first skate party, I was thirty years old. I had never been to Atlanta, a mere four-hour drive from Nashville. Skate parties helped me realize I wanted my children to travel anywhere in the world they wanted to. I wanted to expose them to people who loved doing something as a unit and had such an exciting time doing so. I wanted them to see friendships and celebrations.

No doubt, the best aspect of skating parties is the relationships you form there. In 2007, Dee and I traveled to North Carolina for Rolling in the Carolina's Jam. We met this random guy who was cutting up more than Dee at the meet-n-greet. He introduced himself—we talked, laughed, and didn't stop laughing. The next thing I knew, I invited him to our first wedding anniversary at our local skating rink in Nashville.

"Girl," he said. "Tennessee is pretty far from where I live, and I don't even know you like that. I'm still trying to figure out if I even like y'all or not!"

We all laughed and went to the rink. What that man did in his skates was astonishing. I had never seen anything like it in all my life. Here was this man in a tuxedo and top hat rolling with mad skills I didn't even know existed. I was speechless.

At the end of the weekend, everyone was taking photos. While saying their, "see-you-next-times." That's when he came over to us. He and Dee exchanged numbers and dapped it up. Then he looked at me. "Hey country girl," he said, "I don't know if I can swing that trip to Nashville but congrats on your anniversary.

"I understand," I said and never expected to see him again.

Finally, the big weekend had arrived and I was STRESSED OUT! We had such a big event planned, it had cost us so much money, and we had no idea if anyone was even going to show up!

"Sis, look," Meme said, "I love you and so many people love you and Dee. You don't have to worry about who shows up or not." She wiped my tears and looked me in the eye. "Now get yourself together. You can't look crazy in front of your guests." We laughed, hugged, and went to the welcome event at the recreation center.

My phone rang. I was unsure of the number but knew it wasn't local.

The sweetest voice said, "Hey sis, this is Trishtina. We need directions to where you are?"

Yes, ATL's own Ms. Jive Biscuit had come to support us! That call changed all the craziness I was feeling. I finally felt like myself again.

Minutes later, the music was booming, and Meme was teaching Chicago-style stepping. My back was to the door, so I had no idea who tapped on my shoulder mid-dance step. I turned to see it was the infamous ICE from Philly. I broke down crying. My perfect makeup was all over my face, I cried so much. When people travel hundreds of miles for a milestone in your life—to celebrate you, and the one you love while asking for nothing in return—that is a privilege. It is something to be grateful for.

A year after our wedding, Dee and I announced we'd soon have a new family member. Yes, we were pregnant! No, it did not stop me from going on skate trips even though my skate family refused to let me roll. It didn't stop my fun. Traveling to see all my friends was great, and I could skate at home. I'd gotten a doctor's note permitting me to skate. There was this one skater, Shawn, who protected me when I was out on the skate floor.

"Hey!" he'd shout at anyone who got within a foot of me and Dee. "Watch out for her! She is pregnant!"

He begged Dee to make me sit down, but Dee would shake his head and say, "I appreciate you, man, but she is good."

I was due May 15th, but Baby Demitrius had different plans. April 23rd was the day he selected to come out. We received gifts from skaters all over, and he continued to receive gifts from them his whole first year of life. At twelve weeks old, Demitrius Jr AKA DJ packed up for his first road trip. We headed to the Louisville Rail Ridaz skate party. The moment we entered the rink, DJ had countless new uncles and aunts. To this day, DJ loves going to skate parties with us to see his skate family.

Losing a family member is never easy. When DJ was a toddler, about to turn a year old, I lost my lifeline. The one that gifted me with life. My momma was gone, two days before my third wedding anniversary. I had spent the night with her in her hospital room. I knew she was sick, and the doctors tried to prepare us, but there is no way to prepare for such a thing. I had to figure out how to accept it.

The next morning, when I opened my eyes, I knew I had to get it together and take care of business. My life hadn't stopped because my mothers had. I headed to Walmart to get some errands finished and get my mind off things.

A call came in as I was heading to the checkout, but the number did not look familiar.

"Hello?"

"Can I speak with Denise?"

"This is her. Who is this?"

"This is Joi from Atlanta."

I stopped in my tracks. I couldn't believe it. Madame Queen of the South, Joi, the legend of Skate-a-thon, had called to check on me. My mom had nothing to worry about. Her baby girl had family showing up to make sure everything was ok. For weeks, I received calls, emails, and even money from skaters I knew and some I did not. We were all family all the same. Steve of the Rail Ridaz drove three hours for mama's funeral. The Dogg Pound sent cards and many other clubs and individuals too. Each card addressed for me and my family showing their love, condolences, and support. I couldn't believe it, after seventeen years in the skate world, I've seen it time and time again.

I am grateful for my skating family. They bring me so much joy and good times. It allowed me to meet an amazing man, a friend to this day. I can say with pride, I am so in LIKE with him! My boyfriend, my husband, my Rolla/Dude, Dee! We have a true expansion of countless friendships, and support. It was a dear sister in this beautiful family, Nikki Bowens-Robinson who planted the seed of my first book. It is about my second coming-of-age through roller skating and along the way, rolling in love. Love Roll Lifetime: The Unforeseen Journey.

Life can't always be roses. Sometimes it has thorns and thistles. Continue to nurture the rose, it always blooms. We continue to thank God for his master plan having us to MEET ON THE WOOD and ROLL UNTIL...

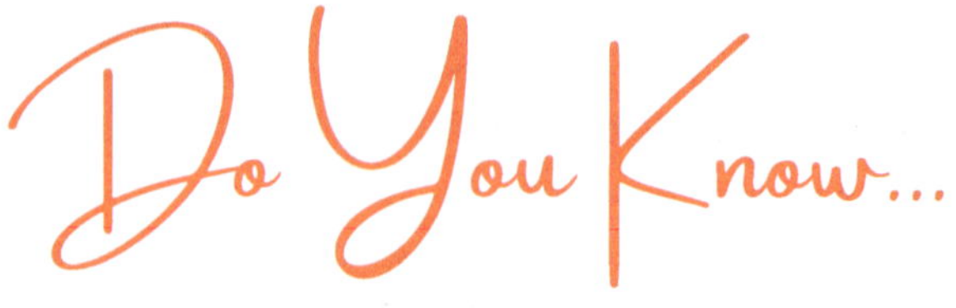

That Roller Skating Helps Your Balance?

Roller skating not only enhances your cardiovascular health but also contributes significantly to improving your balance. When you skate, you engage various muscle groups, including your lower-back and abdominal muscles, to propel yourself forward and backward. This continuous motion challenges your core muscles, requiring you to maintain a steady and stable center of gravity to remain upright. By consistently practicing roller skating, you can strengthen these core muscles, leading to improved balance and stability not only on skates but also in your daily life activities. So, lace up those skates and roll your way to better balance and overall physical well-being!

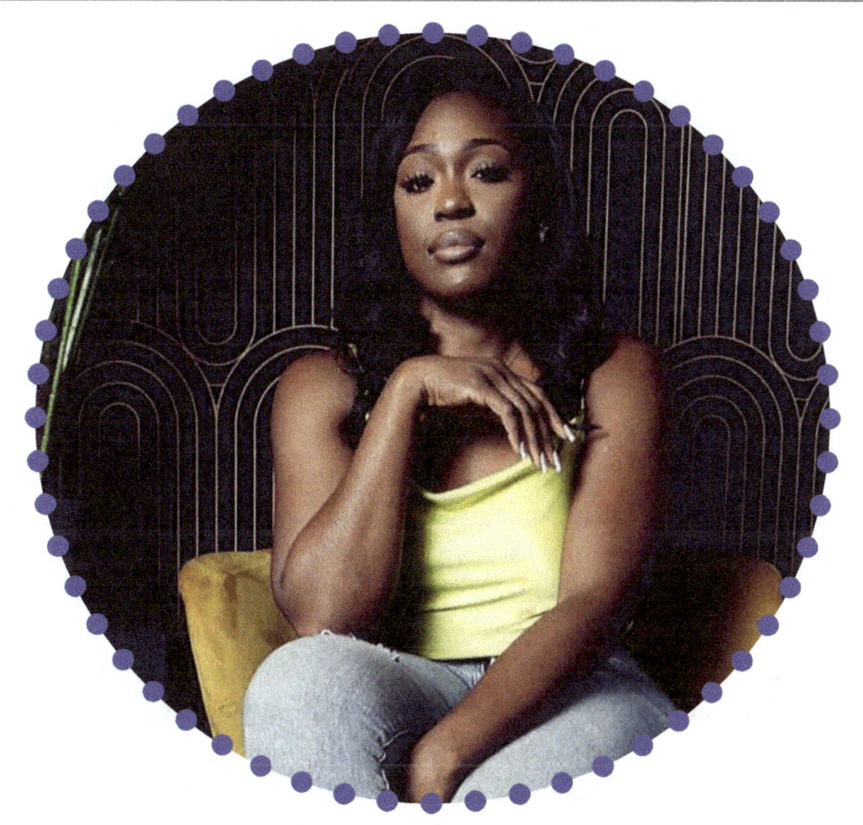

Letticia Etti

aka Lola

Facebook: Letticia Lola Etti | Instragram: tishtisha

"Student for Life"

Without skating, I don't know what life would be like for me. I am grateful to have this hobby, yet even more grateful for the teachers I have had. I've learned so much about myself, and crazy enough, this hobby has also shown me I still have so much to learn as well.

When I was six or seven, my mom would take me and my youngest brother to the skating rinks in Florence, SC, every Sunday. It was our family night, even though we were already a very tight-knit family.

At that age, skating was fun! Something to do like any other kid at that time. What made skating begin to stand apart for me was seeing my mom roll! Even though she doesn't skate anymore, I remember her skates hitting the dark wooden floor. She would turn around and skate backward—all night without missing a beat. To a young Lola, it was one of the most mesmerizing things I could witness. Yeah, I get it from my mama!

As time passed, life happened. I began to take interest in many other things, such as sports and furthering my education. This pushed skating to the back of my life for the next couple of years. My family then moved to Jacksonville, FL. Jacksonville was the first big city I lived in. It was a complete culture shock for me. Yet, I graduated high school and received a full scholarship to the University of Florida, where I earned my bachelor's in Industrial and Systems Engineering. The school was tough, and I looked for many outlets from the long nights of studying. That's where I started taking an interest in Gainesville's local rinks. Still didn't care about skating that much, but I started thinking of it more. Finally, I graduated from college and was ready to take on the world.

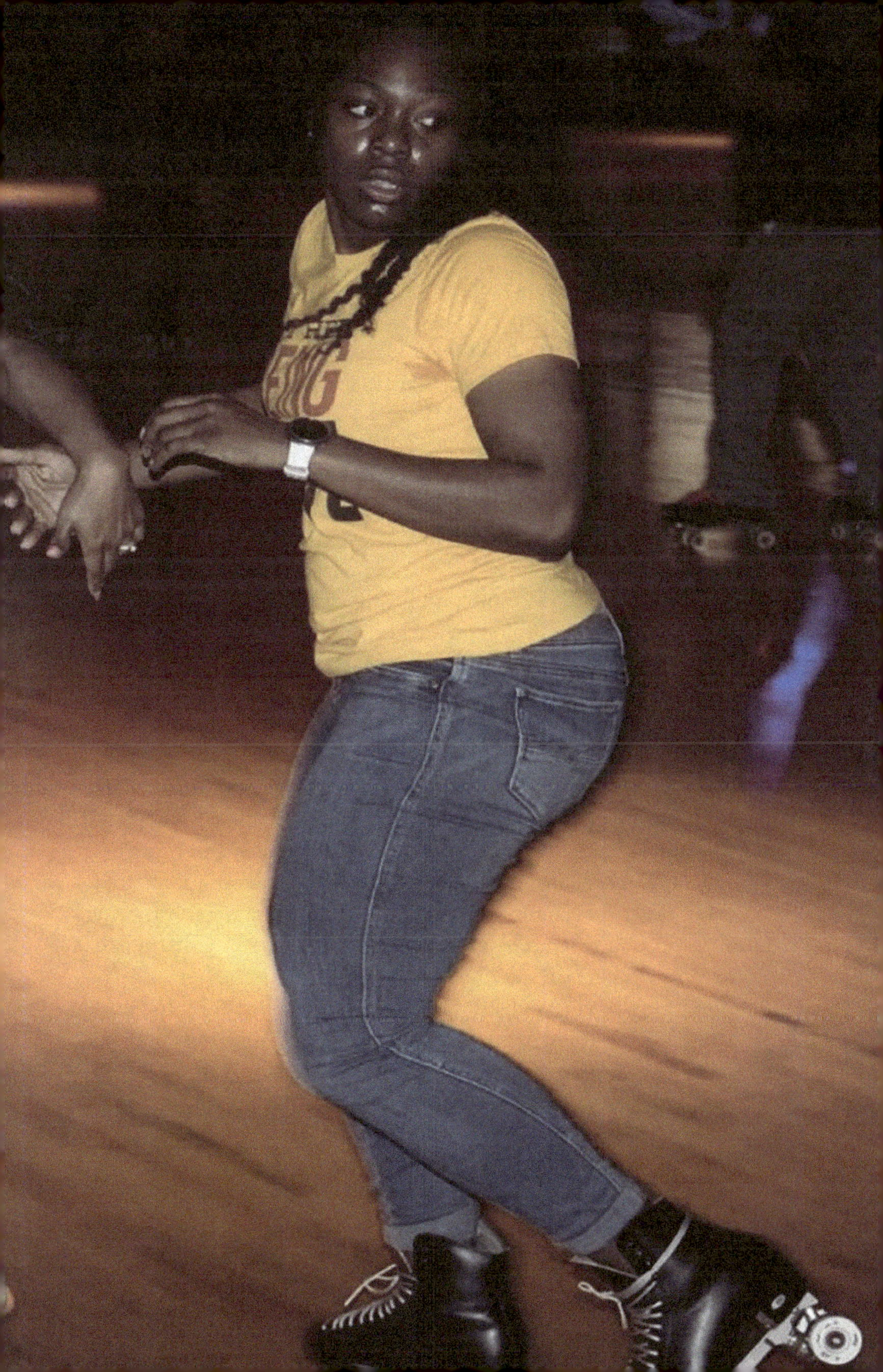

As I prepared to begin my career, skating helped me transition into real work. I enjoyed visiting the rinks and having fun. Skating made me feel like a kid again, in ways I hadn't felt before.

I got an offer as an Engineer for Delta Airlines and moved to Atlanta. Skating was now something I liked to do but not as a big priority, but that soon changed.

The first rink I ever visited was Golden Glide since moving to Decatur, Georgia. It was also the first rink I learned to skate in. This rink holds a very sentimental place in my heart; Sundays were my night. I would look forward to it all week. One Sunday, I decided to go there at the last minute, which is where my life changed.

Skating for me summed up three stages, broken down by the teachers that taught me what I now know. The first stage is from a man named Eric.

Eric was smooth, rhythmic, and a friendly person. That night I decided to go to Golden Glide on a whim, he came up to me and asked me if I wanted to learn how to skate. "Heck yeah!" I told him. For the next year, he taught me how to turn, pivot, and skate to the beat of the music. I'm not even going to lie, I had no rhythm, but I could stand on my two feet on skates. But every Friday and Sunday, Eric had lots of patience working with me, and after months, I started to get it. After that, I caught on so fast. He opened what skating could be as an adult. I became hooked. He helped blend skating and music and how fun it can all be. He invested in my potential, and I am so grateful for that.

As I got better, I caught the eyes of other known skaters. This brings me to the second teacher. Along with the next phase of skating that had the most impact on me.

Gloria Downs is a well-known prolific skater. She took me under her wing and taught me everything that she knew. She taught me how to be passionate, energetic, and fear no one on skates. I was a force to be reckoned with! I also began to become well known across the United States. Gloria and I became the best of friends, which made her teaching me a very tight bond. At that time, Gloria wasn't as big of a teacher as she is today. Even at that time if you didn't have a hard work ethic, no fear of falling, and too cute to sweat she wasn't the teacher for you.

"If you're not falling, then you're not learning," she would say.

What keeps me going is the challenge that learning new things brings. It is what drives me.

As I grew into myself skating, so did my career. Which made managing my professional and skating life a challenge. Many people could not understand the commitments and sacrifices that I had to make. Distancing myself for a while was tough; I had to create balance like many others have to with what they have to do and what they want to do. My will to skate and ambition in my career needed work and over time I learned that balance. That balance is forever changing and to protect my love for skating—I will adjust.

In the midst of a growing career, I met the most pivotal teacher of them all. Bill 'Jamma' Butler the Godfather of Roller Disco, the last and most current stage in my life as a skater. Like many, Bill Butler was a mere myth until one day, one of his students introduced me to him.

At the time, I don't believe Bill Butler remembered my name. He referred to me as the girl in the yellow hat, which was what I was wearing when I met him. He, like all my other teachers, took a chance and began teaching me the Jammin' technique.

The Jammin' technique is a unique style of skate. It encompasses the meticulous movement of your feet and arms, with music and dance. Many of the styles today encompass small bits of the Jammin' technique. It takes years to master this style, and I was up for the challenge.

Always remember when you skate:

Space + The Beat = What You do with Your Feet

As confident as I was skating at that time. In my first session with Mr. Butler, I fell clean on my butt after he instructed me to execute a move. Without saying a word, he grabbed a pair of wrist braces, told me to put them on, and said he would let me know when I can remove them. I wore those braces for four months.

I committed myself to learn this technique four to five days a week, the majority of the time with no music for years. It changed me for the better. I looked at skating from a different perspective. I was better for it.

Mr. Butler serves as a father figure to me. He has taught me several lessons about life through his technique. While all my other teachers taught me valuable lessons. Mr. Butler taught me precision, THE STRIDE, footwork, and musicality. Most importantly, he taught me how to find myself. The sky is the limit when you skate the technique designed for you to add on to it and not to emulate others. You must always reinvent yourself with it. I love it.

I love learning and challenging myself.

It has blessed me to be on this journey with skating and to be a student of so many amazing teachers.

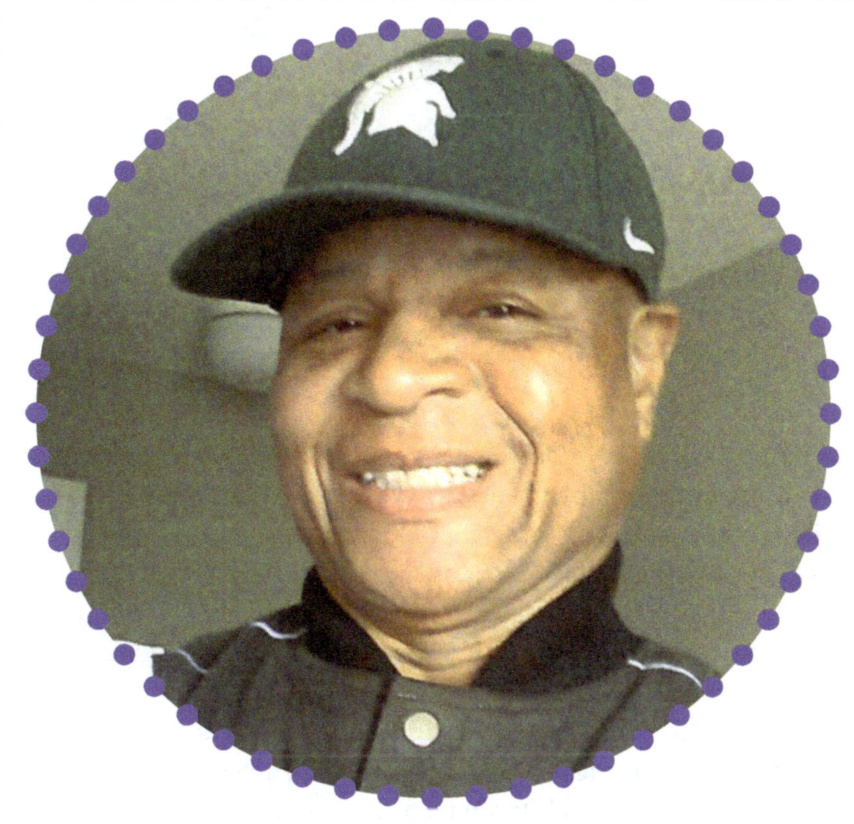

Joe Carter

aka ShowStopper

Facebook: @Joe Carter

"My Roller Skating Story"

I'm a proud member of one of the greatest generations in the history of this nation: the Baby Boomers! We changed the world in so many positive ways, and we saw and experienced so many things growing up, starting in the 1960s: the Vietnam War, Civil Rights Movement, the Cuban Missile Crisis, the first man on the Moon, the first commerical Satellite, and unfortunately, the assassinations of President John F. Kennedy, Dr. Martin Luther King, Jr., and Malcolm X, as well as many other events. The world was so different in those days.

I grew up in Lansing, Michigan. Back then, it was safe to leave your doors unlocked at night, children respected elders, and butt-whippings were standard procedure when you acted up. Wannabe doo-wop groups stood on corners, singing as if they were The Temptations, Blue Magic, or other soulful R&B groups of the time. We played street football, baseball, basketball, went fishing, rode bikes, swam in the river, played board games like Monopoly, and ran all day in the summer. But you had better be on the porch when the street lights came on, or your behind was going to get torn up when you got home. Our parents raised us with respect and discipline, and today, I remain disciplined in every area of my life. I thank God for having strict parents, especially my mama, who did not believe in kids being out of control—period!

In January 1960 at seven years old, my mom let me go to Edru Skating Rink with my best friend Avery and his sister Valerie. It was his birthday, and his mom took us. It was my very first time in a roller skating rink. Little did I know the impact that day would have on my life. And the story begins...

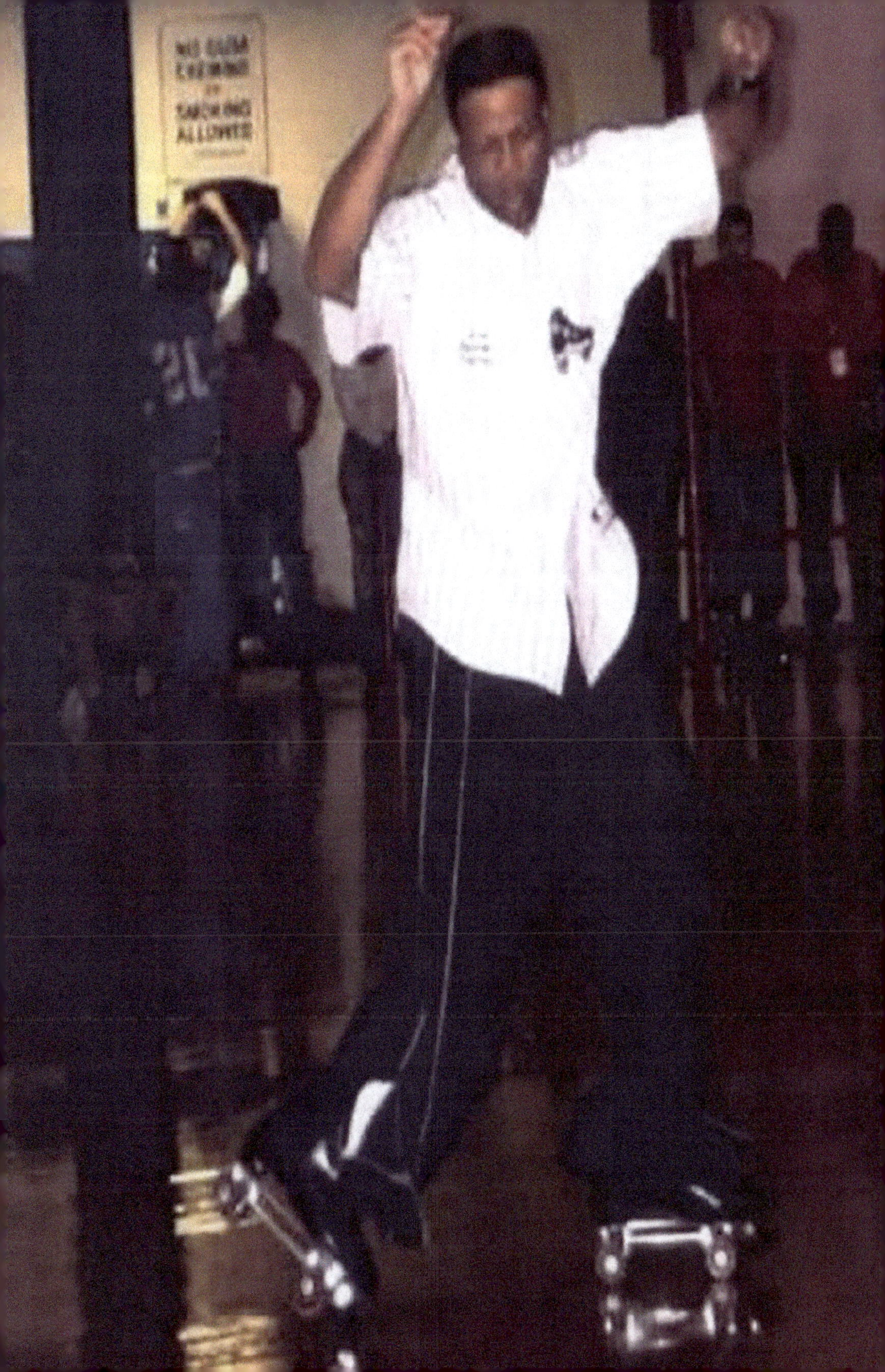

My introduction to skating on a wooden floor happened at Edru. The shiny new surface seemed enormous compared to my previous experiences skating outdoors on sidewalks with old metal strap-on skates. When I tried on the rental skates, I found them restrictive. Preferring comfort, I only tied them halfway up with the tongues down, avoiding pressure on my ankles. However, Mr. Corr, the rink owner, had strict rules, one of which required everyone to tie their skates up to the very top. Unaware of this, I ventured onto the floor. Initially, I managed okay for the first five yards, but then disaster struck. I fell three times in rapid succession—first on my own, then due to a collision with another skater, and finally, causing four more people to fall over me.

Mr. Corr and his floor guards stood over me, and shining a flashlight on me saying, "You! To the Training Strip, and tie those skates all the way up!" After helping me to the Training Strip, which was an area designated just for beginners off the main floor, he pointed at me and said, "Don't come back on the floor until you learn how to skate, by practicing on the Training Strip."

By the summer of 1960, I became a decent enough skater that Mr. Corr allowed me off the Training Strip and onto the main floor. So, I was learning, but he stayed on me every time he caught me with my tongues down on my skates, and not tied up to the top. Eventually, my introduction to other rinks—the Palomar in Lansing, Rollatorium in Jackson, Arcadia in Detroit—became more frequent. I was getting older, stronger, more knowledgeable, and better as a skater. It was in 1969 when I was sixteen years old that I returned to Edru during the teenage and more advanced sessions.

One day, I confidently displayed several flashy and challenging moves on the floor after being challenged by some confident teenagers. Afterward, I took a breather on the sidelines, standing near the Training Strip that I had once despised. It was then that Mr. Corr approached me on his skates, inquiring about my background, including my name, hometown, and skating experience. I introduced myself and mentioned that I had grown up skating at Edru. However, due to my sporadic visits over the years, he didn't recognize me at first. He then said, "Well, you're one of the best damn skaters I've seen in this town." That was enough for me. I didn't gloat or get cocky about it.

I felt a sense of satisfaction and accomplishment. Mr. Corr acknowledged my skill as a skater, and his smile conveyed his recognition. It was a rare moment because, in all my sixty-one years of skating at Edru, it was the only time I saw him smile. From then on, we always greeted each other with mutual respect whenever I skated there. Sadly, Mr. Corr passed away in his 90s several years ago. I will forever be grateful for his dedication and love in maintaining Edru so impeccably. Without him, Lansing wouldn't have had a rink. Thank you, Mr. Corr. Rest in peace.

In 1970, I fell in love with roller skating, finding it both physically and mentally uplifting. It's also when I invented my signature move: the 'Rolls Royce Kick.' Skating is my passion, igniting my creativity and driving me to be innovate. I'll skate to any music and have even practiced without it when necessary. While I favor old school R&B, I've skated to classical to pop, rock, rap, hip hop, jazz, and even country western.

The 1970s stand out as my favorite decade of skating. Michigan's rinks were bustling, especially during adult and R&B sessions. I frequented several favorites like Rollettes in Flint, Rolladium in Pontiac, and Royal Skateland in Detroit. During this time, I was immersed in Detroit's skating style, admiring its intricate footwork and flashy moves. While I developed my own style, I drew inspiration from Detroit and Flint skaters, incorporating some of their moves. Rolladium on Sunday nights and Rollettes in Flint on Wednesdays were hubs for skaters, where I made lasting friendships with fellow enthusiasts like Rockin' Richard, Cynthia Travis, and many others who left a lasting impression on me.

Memories flood back from those skating days, especially the hilarious aftermath of sessions where the dust from wheels and floors would turn our big Afros brown. My buddy Tony Jackson and I sported massive Afros, which always brought a laugh. Skating in Pontiac, Detroit, and Flint meant understanding the risks; on sessions like Trios and Foursomes or Men Only, it was fast and furious—dangerous if you weren't careful. Some skaters wore Pom Poms on their skates, while others rocked processed permed hairdos. Bell-bottom pants were all the rage. In Pontiac, DJ Melvin spun hits like "Shotgun" and "Sugar Hips," igniting the floor with energy. We'd slide, split, jump, kick—every move seemed electrifying. Each rink had its allure, and I made it a point to hit as many as possible weekly. Edru, my home rink, hosted a sizzling Soul Night session on Wednesdays, a tradition that sadly fizzled out in the early '70s.

I dedicated myself to practicing, inventing new skating moves, and participating in competitions. In 1978, I clinched a victory in a city-wide talent contest that featured seventy-seven diverse contestants, ranging from fire breathers to singers, magicians, dancers, and more. I also secured wins in various cities and landed second place in a few competitions. One standout memory is skating in Los Angeles at a venue where you rolled down ramps onto the floor—a thrilling experience, although the rink's name escapes me. While there, locals urged me to pursue television skating, a suggestion I found amusing since my trip was solely for leisure. Nonetheless, I relished the opportunity and even skated outdoors in Venice Beach, California. Despite occasional performances, opportunities for skaters to showcase on TV or at national events were scarce during those years. It wasn't until 2000 that doors began opening for skaters nationwide, fostering connections among enthusiasts like myself.

Around 2003, I began attending National Parties, including Joi's SK8-A-Thon, Rollin in the Carolinas, Independence Roll in Chicago, Icy Hot in Louisville, Kansas City events, SoulSkate Detroit, and gatherings in Cincinnati, Alabama, Washington, DC, and more. I've skated in forty-two states and two Canadian provinces. I had plans to skate in Tokyo, Japan, in 2020 at the Tokyo Dome, but the event was canceled due to COVID-19. The 2000s brought numerous skating-related opportunities and achievements. Earlier, I mentioned my signature move, 'The Rolls Royce Kick,' which I developed in 1970. I named it for its smooth, classy, and timeless qualities, akin to a Rolls Royce. Mastering it was a challenge, requiring precision and balance—I fell around twenty times while learning it over two weeks of daily practice. The move begins with me rotating on my left foot while kicking straight out with the right foot, each kick turning me a quarter of a circle. Rotation and centrifugal force keep the motion fluid. After six to eight quarter turns, I quickly spin on all eight wheels, then transition into a high karate kick with my left foot while rising on my right. It's a move that garners much interest among skaters, but it's crucial to execute it correctly to avoid injury.

In January 2010, I underwent total left knee replacement surgery after two years of persistent pain. The pain became unbearable, even with four Motrin tablets just to skate. Two doctors confirmed I had no cartilage left, leaving me bone on bone. Knee replacement was my only option. Between consultations, I prayed for guidance and found Dr. Mesko, a specialized knee surgeon in Lansing. His card expressed a belief in healing through prayer and the Holy Spirit, confirming my decision. After intense five-month rehab, including extensive exercises and tasks, I returned to skating in June, defying doubts from some skaters. Eleven years later, at sixty-eight, I skate pain-free, disproving skepticism about skating post-surgery. My knee replacement was one of my best decisions, allowing me to continue enjoying skating. I believe in giving back to skating, whether through teaching, promoting, or fostering humility and respect among skaters. Roller-skating has blessed me immensely, and I strive to represent the skating community with excellence and humility at every opportunity.

Throughout my skating career, it's been a true blessing to share the skate floor with thousands of talented skaters like Rockin' Richard Houston, Reggie Gunn, the late great Mr. Charles, Cynthia Travis, Debra Malone, Trenaye Neequaye, Edward "One of a Kind" Reese, D-Nell Reckless, Dave and the Microstars, Ice From Philly, Tex (deceased), Linda Corley (deceased), Lisa McFadden, Richard and Peaches Manning, William, Angela, Richard Humphrey, Josh Smith, Darius D-Breez, Myesha, Chi-Force, JB Elite, Chicago's Most Wanted, Karl Parker (my protege), my brother Ron Carter, D-Nice, Pooh, Kojak Anderson, Terron Frank, and Bobby.

Favorite skating videographers—Bill Washington, who has taken more than two thousand pictures of me over the years, and the incomparable John Smith. Favorite DJs—Big Bob, DJ Joe Bowen, DJ Narcissistic, DJ Wild Child, DJ Arson, DJ Ken Smalls, and DJ Al.

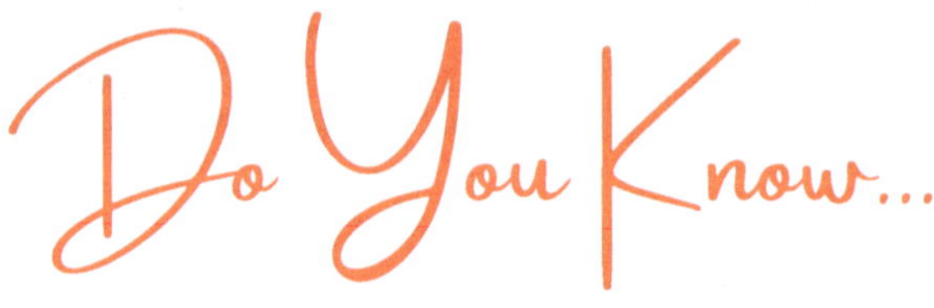

Roller Skating Has Its Own Governing Body?

The International Roller Sports Federation (FIRS) is the worldwide governing body for roller sports. It was founded in 1924 and is recognized by the International Olympic Committee (IOC) as the governing body for roller sports, representing over 100 national federations.

FIRS oversees various disciplines of roller sports, including artistic roller skating, speed roller skating, roller hockey, and roller derby.

FIRS organizes and sanctions international competitions, including world championships and continental championships, for each of these disciplines. It also establishes rules and regulations governing the sport, promotes participation and development at all levels, and works to advance roller sports globally.

In addition to its role in organizing competitions, FIRS advocates for the inclusion of roller sports in major multi-sport events, such as the Olympics, and collaborates with national federations, athletes, and stakeholders to promote the growth and recognition of roller sports worldwide.

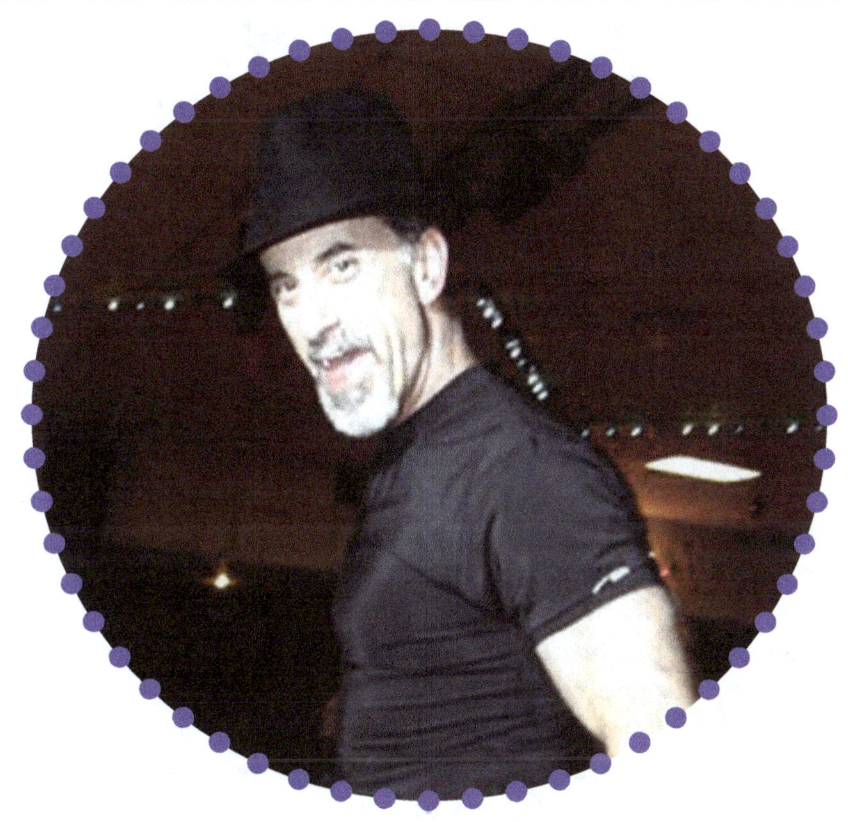

David Walter

Facebook: @David Walter | Instagram: @davidjwalter1

“Known for My Signature Move”

In 1961, when I was about four years old, I got clamp-on skates, and my sister, who is six years older than me, took me outside on the sidewalk. She showed me how to put a skate on and told me to put the other on myself. She had skated before and started skating up and down the sidewalk while I put the other skate on. I used a telephone pole to help me stand up. I was in a pair of shorts and no shirt. No sooner had I let go of the pole, my skates went right out from under me. I desperately grabbed the pole and slid to the ground! Splinters everywhere, it was ugly! I never skated with those clamp-on skates again.

I did not skate again until I was sixteen. I watched people ice skate in person and on TV and always loved it. In 1973, when I was sixteen, my friends, who were all three years older than me, said, “We were going roller skating.” I said, “Not me,” and refused to go. There were three or four of them and even though I was the alpha male of the bunch, they physically grabbed me and forced me into the car. I said, “Fine, but I am not skating.” When we got to the rink, they convinced me to try it. Have you ever seen someone trying way too hard to skate with no finesse? Well, that was me! I fell three to four times before I hit the floor! And when I hit the floor, I hit the floor! Over and over again. I just could not even keep my feet underneath me!

After a few weeks, I learned to push with one foot only as I had ridden a skateboard before, but it was six months of weekly skating before I could push with the other foot! It took two years to learn

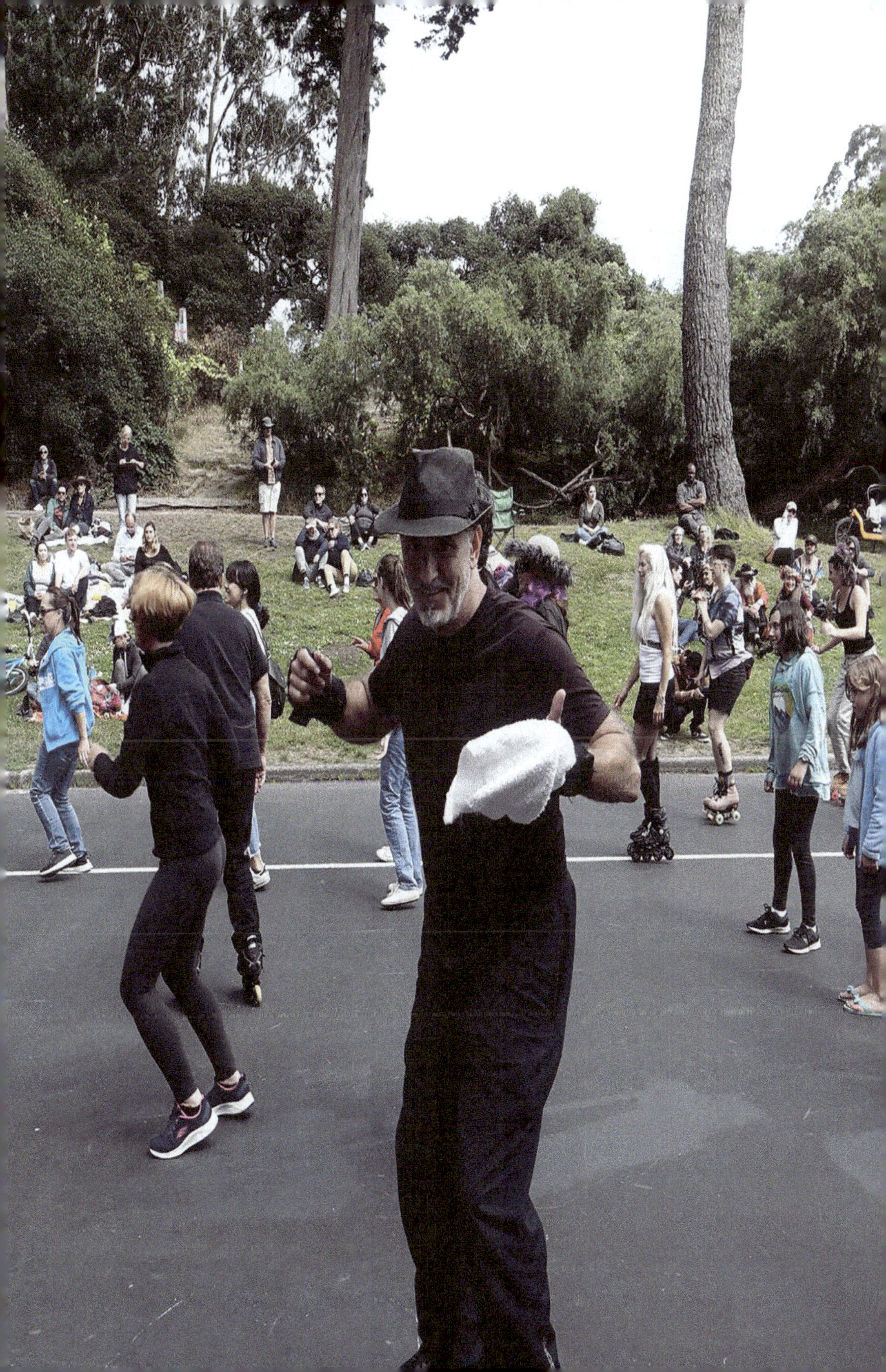

backward. I remember one reason I stayed with it was one time—I think the second time—I had fallen hard, and while I was laying on the floor, a little girl skated up to me, smiled, did a spin, and skated off backward! I said to myself, "That's it! I'm going to learn this or die trying!"

Fast forward five years and I am the only one of the original group who is still skating. I was the best skater at the rink by that time. It was a lonely time in my life as my girlfriend had left me three years earlier and my friends were no longer skating. Since they were older than me, they had moved on and started their lives. I was "stuck" in life, but I had my skating and was proud that I had learned to do it. Then my father died unexpectedly. My parents split when I was two. I was not as close to my dad, as I was to my mom as I lived with her most of the time. I never had the opportunity to show him my "art" of skating and it was very sad for me. I remember going to the rink the next night and saying to myself, "He is watching." It was at that point that I dedicated my life to skating. His death and the fact that I had learned to skate so well served to not only convince me to dedicate myself to skating but also gave me confidence in all areas in my life going forward! The stage was set!

It's 1978, and I was in San Bruno, California, at a family dinner at my sister's house and I said, "I'm going to find a rink to skate at tonight." I looked in the phone book, as there was no Internet back then, and found a rink named Grand Arena in South San Francisco, which I thought was cool as my home rink at the time was Skate Arena in Sunnyvale, about forty miles away. So, I go to Grand Arena that night and peeked in the door and saw two hundred plus rolling and realized I would be the only white person in the house! *Gulp!*

When I was young (kindergarten through fourth grade), I lived in East Palo Alto, which at the time meant that I was the only white kid in a school of four hundred plus, so I had some experience being the only white person, but it had been a while.

So, lace up and as soon as I hit the floor, I've got two, eighteen- to nineteen-year-old guys following me, and they were not trying to make friends, it was more…well, to not make friends, if you know what I mean. I solved that by pulling out a joint and we became friends instantly. That night was super important though as I met several folks who are still friends today. One of them is Richard Humphrey, The Rollerdance Man. He said, "I heard people are skating in Golden Gate Park in San Francisco and think I am going to check it out tomorrow. Would you be interested?" I said I was and met him the next day at the park. For both of us, it was our first time skating at the park! At that time there were thousands of people renting skates from trucks parked just outside the park, so there were lots of people skating, but Richard and I were the only skaters that knew how to do anything. We started making up routines and people were so impressed! We would meet every Sunday and what fun we had! I was known for my signature move—The Coffin—but not anymore as I tore my leg three-quarter of the way in half (quad all the way off at the kneecap), along with more injuries than anyone I know of in skating. If you are wondering, see the Skate Critic's (Ginger and I go back a long way) question: "Have you ever broken something skating?"

Then a radio station, KSFX, asked Richard if he could form a skate team. He got other skaters from Grand Arena to join and the KFSX ROLLONS was born. We hated the name as it sounded like deodorant, but that's what the station wanted. We performed all around the Bay Area, opening discos and doing special appearances. We, along with skaters from Los Angeles, including Christopher from Venice, now in Las Vegas, did a TV show pilot that was never shown in the US called *Dancing Wheels* that featured Stephanie Mills, Sylvester, The Unknown Comic, and Natalie Dunn, who was the three-time World Single Women's Freestyle Artistic Champion. After that, the team had split up, leaving Richard and me. He formed The Golden Rollers, a fabulous three-man team that got lots of exposure. And of course, he has done so many shows and performances throughout the years, as well as teaching so many, he remains to this day a very well-known force in the skating scene. I would be remiss not to mention David Miles as he hit the park the year after Richard and me. I owe so much to him as well as he is The Godfather of Skating in San Francisco as well as the Burning Man, and now the new outdoor rink in Oakland. He saved skating in the park forty years ago by forming the Park Skate Patrol and convincing the city to continue to allow and support it, as well as many other contributions to the art.

After Richard started doing The Golden Rollers I met a woman named Diana Haydon. We were partners both on and off the floor and we ended up winning David Miles's annual contest in GG Park three times in a row. She won the women's singles at least once, might be more, I can't remember. I won the men's singles three times. Those were super fun times! Afterward, she went into the early days of women's bodybuilding and did quite well. We had been teaching skating at the Skate Arena in Sunnyvale, but we split up. We are still in touch to this day. Not long after, that rink closed, which was not good for me as my whole life revolved around skating and teaching! The good news is after eleven years of skating there, I found my new home for the next twenty-seven years, from 1984 to 2011, at Cal Skate Milpitas. This is where I taught so many people, young and old, Black and White, and every other shade! Not sure how many people I have taught, but it is in the thousands! In fact, I just had a woman come up to me at an outdoor skate event during the pandemic and said, "You taught me to skate twenty-five years ago at Cal Skate, and you taught my kids, and you taught my grandkids, and you look the same!" That felt good, especially that last part! I stopped charging when I teach long ago as I found that it takes the fun out of it for me. But my favorite was teaching the Tiny Tots class on Saturday mornings at Cal Skate. Two to four hundred kids at a time, and there were several teachers, and we got them rolling! I like to show off on my skates and show how good I am, but I like teaching people even more. That is my Art of Skating. I have been in books, commercials, on TV, in newspapers and magazines and that is great, but If I can give a young person what I got when I was sixteen, which was empowerment, then I feel I am passing on not only skating but something that person may carry forward into their lives in a positive way!

So, if you ever see me rollin', please don't be shy, say hi! See you on the wood (or plastic, or cement, if we must)! And watch out for those Skate Mates!

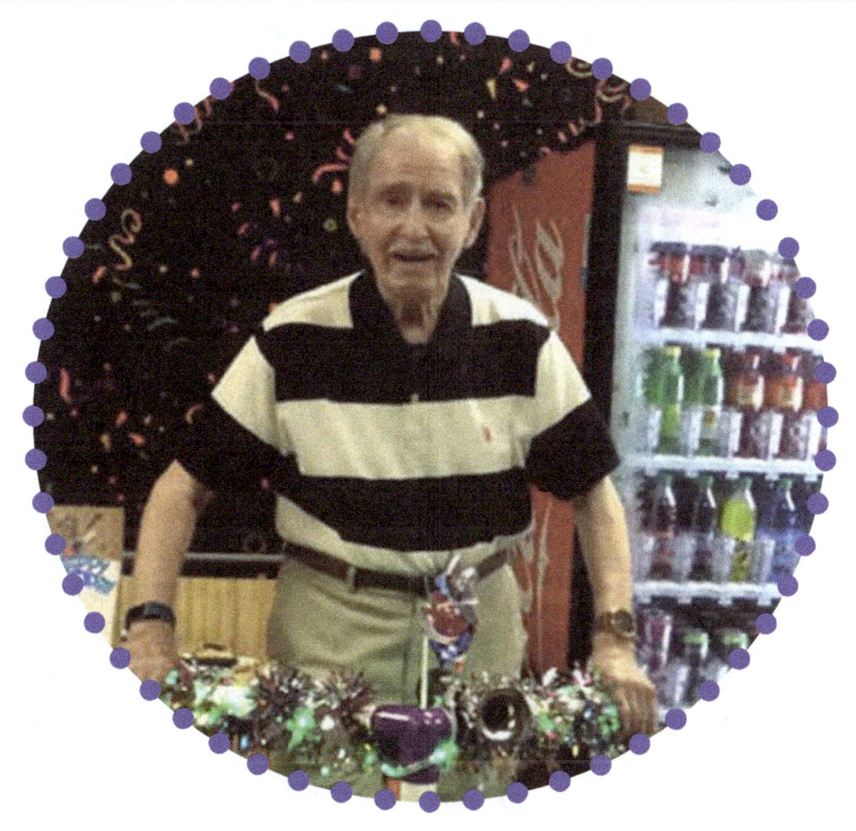

Gene Elliott

Facebook: @Gene Elliott

"The Magic Man of Skateland"

In 1930, roller skating rinks traveled from city to city, staying stay for thirty days before moving on. My mother loved to skate. When I was five, she got me a pair of Union Hardware skates for Christmas. I had my own skate key.

The year was 1942. I did not graduate from high school. My older brothers, Vernon and Norman, were in the Army and we were living in Sumter, South Carolina. My father had a stroke, and they sent him to Duke University Hospital in Durham, North Carolina. To help financially, I quit school and went to work in the sawmill. On my eighteenth birthday, I volunteered for the U.S. Army. I did not want to wait to be drafted. I had seventeen weeks of training and they shipped me off to the Battle of the Bulge in Germany. When the war ended, they sent me back to the USA for special training. I was in California headed to Japan when President Truman dropped the atomic bomb.

In 1947, one night, my brother, Norman, and I were riding around town in my 1935 Ford. We were down in the Highland area of Hickory, North Carolina. We saw on the top of the hill a building under construction and the lights were on. We had heard that a roller skating rink was being built in the area. We went inside and Mom and Pop Frye were still there. This was to be Hilltop Skating Rink. The skating floor was finished, but it was in a mess with timbers and sawdust all over. We had been skating at a rink that had been closed down, so we had our skates. We asked if we could clean the floors so we could skate. The owners said, "Yes, go ahead." We were regulars

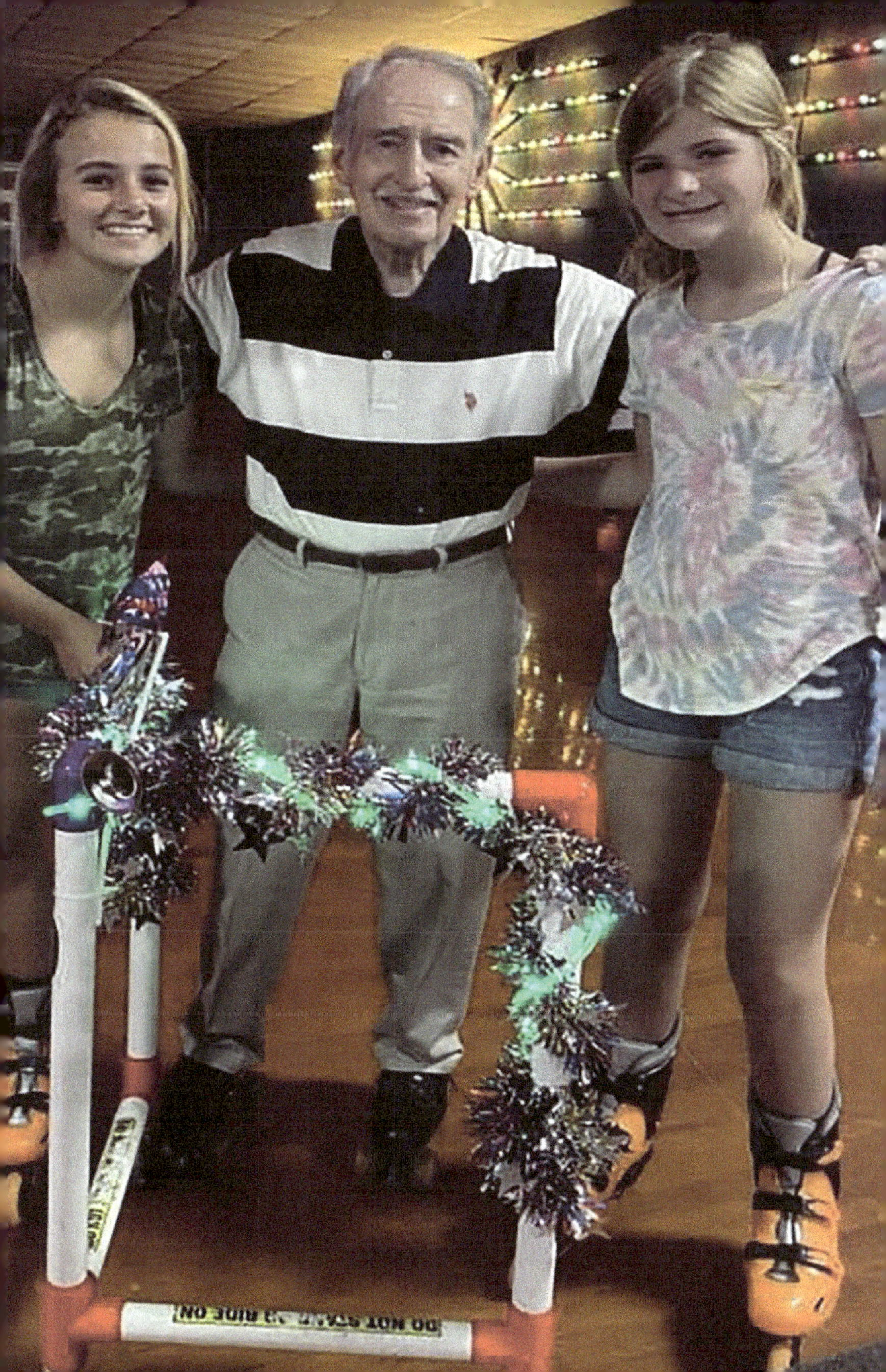

then. We would brag to the others that we were the first to skate at this rink. My son-in-law, Coy Reid, said that he had skated there as a teenager and that he was named Mr. Hilltop. The rink is not there now. The building was torn down. It's a vacant lot. Another one bites the dust.

In 1947, I met my wife, Mary Lee, at the Edgewood Skating Rink in Granite Falls. At first, she wanted nothing to do with me. One of the girls asked her. "Why do you not want to be with Gene?" She replied, "Because he is such a show-off." We were married in 1948 and skating was a big part of our marriage and our family. My wife and I continued skating together for years.

In 2000, Mary Lee had a stroke, and I hung up my skates and was with my wife around the clock, caring for her. She was in the hospital and then in rehab for months. Those times were difficult. I went to all of her rehab classes and learned how to continue her care at home. From her wheelchair, she taught me how to do all the things that she had been doing all these years. I became a pretty good cook. For the next six years, we were closer than we had ever been. We fell in love again. Mary Lee passed away in 2006. We were married for fifty-seven years.

In 1958, I was the parts manager at Hickory Motor Sales, the local Dodge car dealership in Hickory, North Carolina. I was holding down two jobs. When I got off from work, I would get a bite to eat and head out to Edgewood Skating Rink in Granite Falls, North Carolina. It was a small rink. I was the DJ and floor manager on Saturday and Wednesday nights. On Saturday, I would take my 16-mm movie camera and make movies of the skaters, and announce that they would be shown on Wednesday night at the end of the session. We had two sessions on Saturday with large crowds. This really helped the Wednesday night sessions, with many wanting to see themselves skating. We set the movie screen up on the rink floor. Many kids would sit on the floor for a better view. I enjoyed this rink, as we had the couple whistle skate, trios, and the Grand March. We would offer skating contests by age levels and a prize for the winners. This rink had a basement and the business downstairs got too big and the rink needed to expand. So Edgewood moved several miles away.

In 1959, my life could have ended that night. The rink was closed that night because of heavy snow. I called the rink, and the rink manager, Ruth Church, was there cleaning. I went up with my wife, Mary Lee, and daughter, Bunnie. When it was time to leave, they went out to the car. I was skating to "Primrose Lane," by Jerry Butler. One of the fluorescent light bulbs fell to the floor. I was picking up the glass, and the building shook. I thought it was an earthquake. I looked to the right, and the wall had blown out. I could see the house next door. The Holy Spirit picked me up and took me across the rink at a speed I could not have done. I jumped the rail that I could not have done. As the right wall blew out, I could see cars outside. The steel door caught the edge of the roof and I crawled out. The rink had a flat roof and could not support the weight of the snow. I am blessed. I am never alone.

In 1964, my daughter, Bunny Reid, and I were dancing partners. We had six different dances: waltz, tango, skaters, blues, and two others. We mastered the dances. We went to Winston-Salem and entered the competition. This was our first. We got a bronze medal.

I enjoyed skating in the seventies. There was so much great music with all the different recording artists. Disco was here, and I loved it. The Bee Gees had us all "Staying Alive." John Travolta gave us all the "Saturday Night Fever." I was all over the skating rink floor. I had a real live Travolta shirt and a few of his moves. I was ready to "Get Down Tonight." Skateland created a disco atmosphere with the giant silver ball and the flashing colored lights.

As we rolled into the eighties, I was in my late fifties and I was a floor guard at Skateland. In comes Bill Garrett as the new manager. A much younger fellow than me, he came out onto the rink floor to skate. I had never seen anything like it before. He was a freestyle figure skater. Everything in skating has a name. He began to roll, and I watched. He did the Flip, Loop, Mapes, Salchow, and the Axel. It was beautiful to watch as he let it roll. I was glad that I was working there. Bill started teaching classes. Over some time, I was able to do them. The Axel and Salchow were the hardest. At my age, I loved the jumps so much that I added the waltz jump, Russian split, and the grapevine. I could only do one rotation, and today they are doing the quads. There are so many today in their forties and fifties who say they are too old to skate. I tell them they are never too old to skate, and that I teach skating. I am ninety-five years old and rolling two nights a week. Get up off the couch!

In the eighties, I had my love of skating and my love of performing street magic. For years, I went up to Pigeon Forge, Tennessee, for the Gathering of Magicians. There were about three hundred magicians from around the world. For three days, we would perform magic from ten in the morning until ten at night. We all shared our secrets. I would perform my magic tricks on Thursday nights. In the snack bar. Something new each week. I was named The Magic Man of Skateland.

In January 2007, my daughter, Bunny, who was a data manager at Webb Murray Elementary, hosted a skating fundraiser for a school project. Skateland said they would donate a dollar for each student who came to skate. They had one major problem, none of the teachers were skaters. So my daughter asked me if I could help out and I did. This was the first time I had gone skating since my wife had taken ill and eventually passed away. This was what got me back into skating. I was eighty years old at the time and I have skated each week from that day on.

In 2015, I contracted shingles in the face and looked like a monster. I was in the hospital for ten days, not expected to live. During this time, I also lost my memory and could not recognize my son, Barry. I spent six weeks in the nursing home in a wheelchair. A month in home rehab. I had to learn how to walk again. After six months, I was walking up and down the hill to strengthen my legs. I went back to roller skating. My doctor said if it were not for my physical condition, we would not have been having that conversation. I take ten thousand steps a day on my Fitbit.

Later this same year, it was my eighty-ninth birthday. I went skating and when I drove up, there were only two cars in the parking lot. I went into the rink early as Donna Heavner Rhodes, Skateland's manager, let me come in so I did not have to stay outside in the weather and the long lines. Catawba County Deputy Sheriff Dennis Dixon was standing next to the rail alone and they had not yet turned on the rink's lights.

Dennis said, "Gene, I need to show you something in the snack bar."

As we walked into the snack bar, I saw nothing wrong. Suddenly, up jumped my daughter, Bunny Reid, and twenty-some of my grandchildren, great-grandchildren, and great-great-granddaughter, yelling, "Happy Birthday, Papaw!"

Now this took planning. My Thursday night skate buddy, Andy Bruckner, had a birthday cake and a huge birthday card he had been having the skaters sign for weeks. The next surprise was my son-in-law, Cody Reid, who is a sheriff with Catawba County, contacted a reporter friend of his from the Hickory Daily Record wanting my story and some pictures. I thought it would be a small article on page 14. To my surprise, they put the picture on the front page in color. They also delivered a stack of the The Hickory Daily Record to my front door. Donna had the picture of me framed and mounted in the rink lobby and it is still there today.

On Feb. 10, 2017, I got a call one morning from Kristen Hampton of Channel 3 WBTV, an affiliate of CBS. She said, "Are you the Elliott that roller skates?"

"Yes."

"I would like to do a piece on you."

"Now, just what does that consist of?"

"I will meet you at Skateland, take a few pictures, ask a few questions and be out of your way."

She came and stayed over an hour and a half. We had so much fun. She had me doing all kinds of things.

Kristen was in the middle of the rink, interviewing Donna Heavner Rhodes, Manager of Skateland. I skated over.

"Are you tired?" Kristen asked me.

"No."

"Would you skate some more for me? I want this on my phone."

The next morning, I got a phone call from Kristen. "Gene, I am here in the newsroom, and I have never seen so much excitement here over a story. They are loving it. Your story will be on the evening news."

It went viral on CBS. You can see the three-minute video on YouTube: "90 year old shows off moves at skating rink (Hickory NC)." It has 18,600 hits and still climbing.

In 2019, COVID-19 hit and the rinks were closed. I thought my skating days were over. There was no way I could make a comeback six months later. After all, I was ninety-four years old. One morning, I received a phone call from Donna Heavner Rhodes, the manager of Skateland USA. She said, "The rink is closed, but I will be here at the rink from 9:30 a.m. till 1:30 p.m. I am doing a webinar on the office computer. If you would like to, you can come and skate."

Wow, was I happy! She put on the disco music and I had the whole rink to myself. Donna had brought her little black dog, Macee, with her. Macee would jump on the rails and race beside me. She could run as fast as I could skate.

On Tuesday, July 13, 2021, a party was planned for my ninety-fifth birthday at Skateland USA. It had been six years since some of us had been together. So, it was also a reunion. My very good skating buddy, Andy Bruckner, did the planning. Mellissa D. Patton brought the cake and a tee-shirt that read: Guardian Angel. Her daughter, Breanna Carpenter, made the largest card with lights. It was a special night. Tabitha and Brittany Trivette were in the snack bar, serving up the giant pizzas. William Francis Stidam, better known as Sarge, was the DJ. He had a list of my favorite songs. When I got out on the floor, I was back in my seventies. I am not a skater; I am a dancer. He also decorated a skatemate with a fan and a horn. My daughter, Bunny Reid, brought all of my grand, great-grand, and great-great-grandchildren. I often see grandparents come to watch their children skate. My grandchildren get to watch me skate. That's something special! When I am out on the floor, I am never alone. I have my Guardian Angel.

I was spending so much time at Skateland that Bill Garrett hired me as assistant manager, along with Rick Detter and Ronnie Caldwell. The four of us would meet and select a work schedule and plan special events. I drew Easter Monday and all-day skate. It was well promoted. Get a drink, a snack, and drop off the kids. It was a big success. We set a record attendance with nine hundred ninety-three—the largest on record.

I started teaching beginner classes on Monday nights, one hour before the rink opened. The skaters would then stay and skate during the regular session. My class got so large that I had to divide the rink and Bill Garrett would take my overflow. At ninety-five, I am still teaching. I help new skaters each week. I have made so many friends.

I love to meet new skaters. I go to the snack bar. I approach those sitting down. I carry a short piece of rope in my pocket. I say, "Do you see this piece of rope? Well, for the past nine years, I have been offering a dollar to anyone who can tie this rope with one hand in one second." I would let them try, with no success. I then perform the one-hand knot. I have five mind-blowing tricks with ropes. I love to see their faces.

On July 15, 2021, after skating Tuesday Night at the party with so many friends and loved ones, I was ready to come down off of cloud nine. It was July 15, and I was going roller skating. As I drove into Skateland USA's parking lot, I saw Donna Heavner Rhodes standing there with Ron Lee from Channel 3 WBTV an affiliate of CBS.

Ron said, "Let me get you wired up. Everything you do or say for the next two hours will be recorded."

The story went viral; it was shown in New York and Miami within hours. This was a complete surprise. The next surprise I got inside the rink was that Donna had set up Skateland's Birthday Party Room with two giant birthday cakes. Everyone at the rink was invited to the party. They all sang "Happy Birthday." My longtime friend, Kenneth Rhodes, whom I had not seen for years, who was on staff for twenty-nine years, showed up and helped me skate backward. I invited everyone to come back for my one-hundredth birthday.

Last night as I was out walking, I met my neighbor, Amber Summerrow. I started telling her all the things that were going on in my life with surprise birthday, and The Evolution of Skating. She knows of my love of skating.

I said, "I wrote about twenty pages of my story and I wonder how it will end."

Amber said, "Your story is not going to end. You are ninety-five strong and an inspiration to others. I want to go skating. I cannot wait to tell my mother that my neighbor is an author and a legend."

Do You Know...

About Roller Hockey?

Roller hockey is a fast-paced sport played on roller skates, where two teams compete to score goals by shooting a puck into the opposing team's net. Players wear protective gear, including helmets, pads, gloves, and inline roller skates, with goalkeepers equipped with additional protective gear. The game is characterized by continuous action and frequent transitions between offense and defense, with players using hockey sticks to control and shoot the puck. Roller hockey can be played in different variants, including traditional roller hockey and inline hockey, with inline hockey gaining popularity due to its speed and maneuverability. Competitions range from recreational leagues to professional and international tournaments, organized by national governing bodies and overseen by international federations like the International Roller Sports Federation (FIRS). Roller hockey enjoys a strong following worldwide, attracting players of all ages and skill levels.

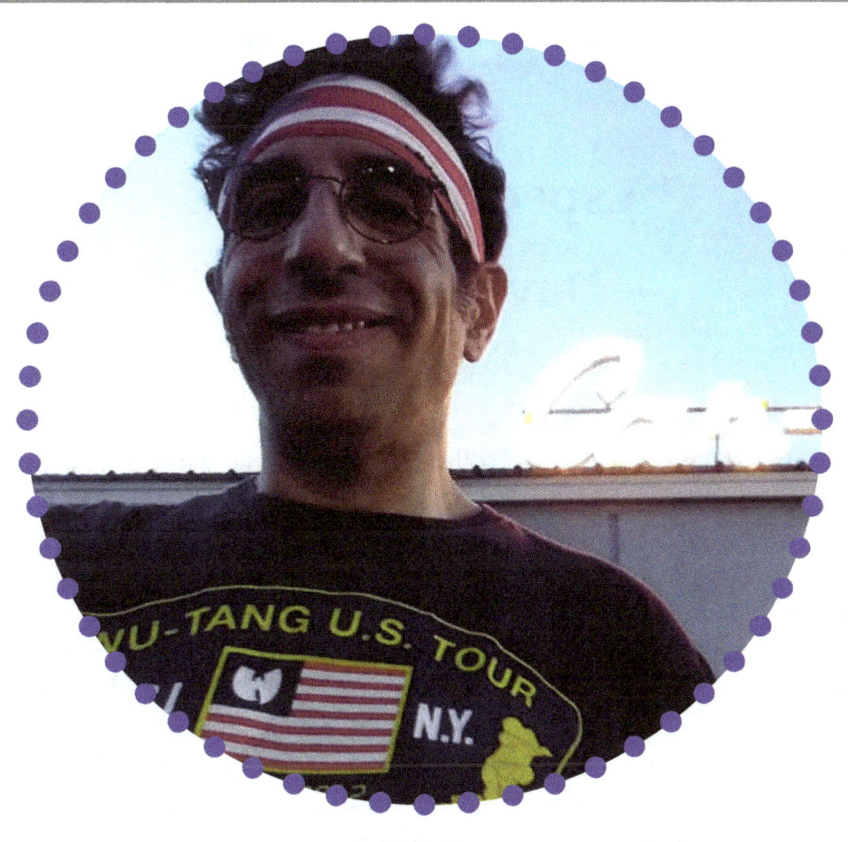

Lee Vasquez

aka Lee McFee

Facebook: @Lee McFee Instagram: @leev.mcfee

“Especially in This Day and Age”

Summarizing six decades of roller skating, especially in a brief chapter, is quite challenging, particularly in today’s era of short attention spans dominated by platforms like TikTok. Yet, it’s through years of experience both outdoors and on hardwood floors that I’ve gained the insight and stability to embrace this challenge and share my journey within the skate culture. It all began innocently enough, like many others, during my middle school years in late ‘70s New York City.

Roller skating ignited a passion within me, coinciding with a peak in skating interest. Unbeknownst to me, this path would be filled with cherished memories and valuable lessons shaping the person I am today. However, as life’s responsibilities took precedence, my focus on skating diminished over time. Marriage, parenthood, and professional pursuits diverted my attention, leading me to halt skating in 2004.

In 2011, a move to Austin, Texas, offered a new pace of life, yet my identity as a skater remained ingrained. Despite the demands of an intense IT job and health concerns, I found myself drawn back to the hardwood in 2015. As of September 2021, six years into my rediscovered passion for skating, I am in the best physical shape of my life, realizing that roller skating transcends mere exercise—it has become a cornerstone of my existence, providing balance amidst life’s complexities.

As I celebrate my 54th trip around the sun, I reflect on my upbringing in NYC—a city pulsating with global fashion and cultural significance. Growing up amidst diverse familial structures and surrounded by colorful personalities, I developed a deep appreciation for individuality and acceptance.

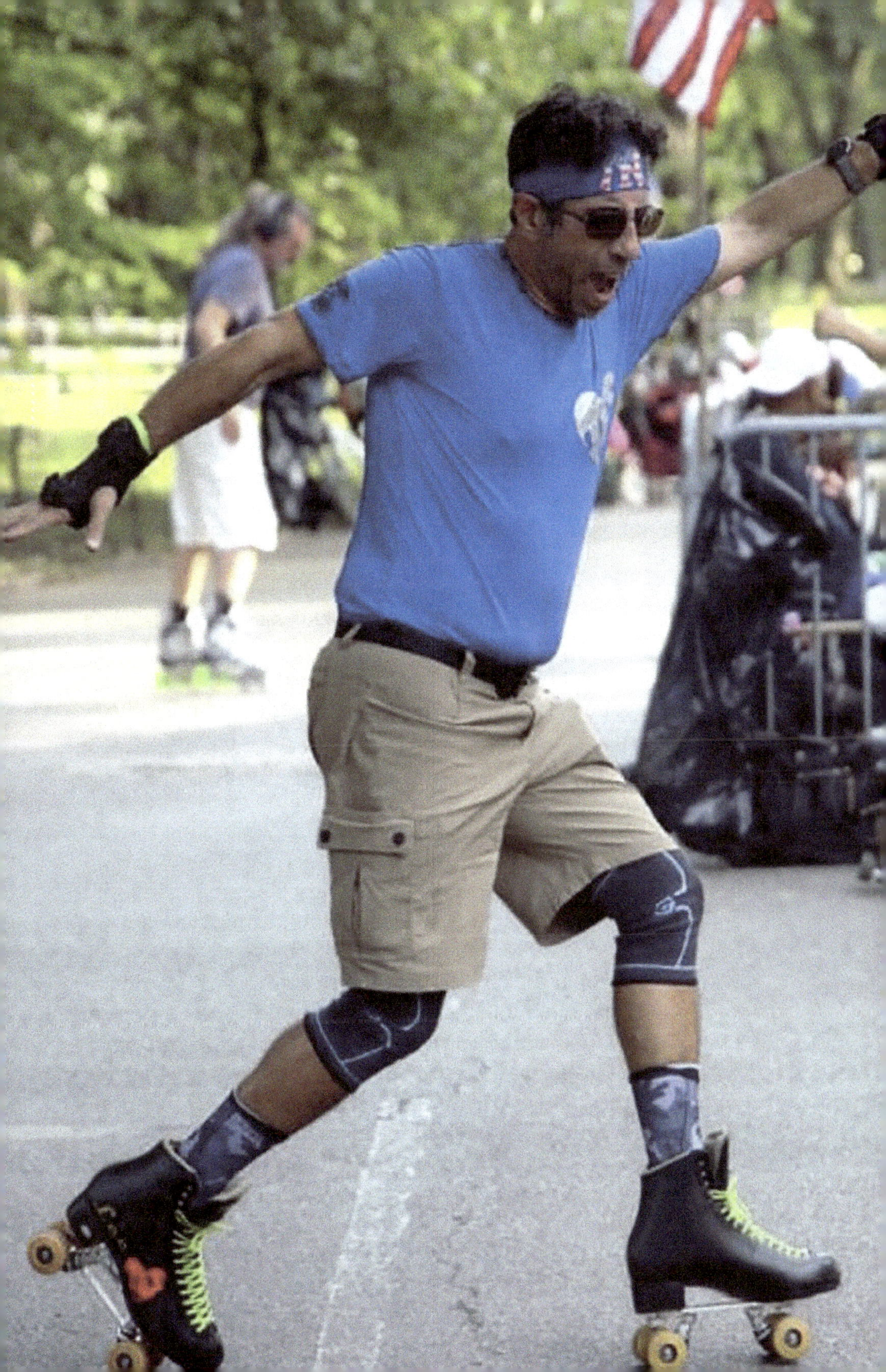

My introduction to roller skating occurred during my middle school years, sparked by witnessing a girl gracefully skating in the courtyard of my apartment building. This inspired me to acquire my first pair of skates and embark on a journey of learning and exploration. Venturing to Central Park allowed me to observe and skate alongside some of the city's finest, including the legendary Bill Butler, whose innovative style melded Detroit roots with NYC disco vibes.

The roller disco scene was a place of transformation, where one's skill on skates mattered more than societal norms. Age, profession, and wealth were overshadowed by the artistry displayed on wheels—a concept that deeply resonated with me as a young man searching for his identity.

Growing up with hardworking parents in a financially tight situation, I became resourceful, taking on off-the-books jobs like delivering pizzas for neighborhood spots such as Tom's and later Jackson Hole. With another skater working alongside me at Jackson Hole, I could fuel my passion for skating.

I stumbled upon High Roller on 57th Street, tucked away in a former parking garage. It was here that I first experienced roller disco, surrounded by quality sound and lighting systems. The atmosphere was electric, with skaters filling the white floor while skate guards kept watch. I was captivated, longing to be part of it all.

Attending the all-ages sessions whenever I could afford it, I formed connections with older kids, finding camaraderie as we journeyed together to the Columbus Circle trains after each session. Little did we know, these connections would lay the groundwork for what we now call our skate family.

Our group mirrored the diversity of the city, comprising individuals from various backgrounds and schools. Despite our differences, we were united by our love for skating. The group was dynamic, with members coming and going based on their level of interest. Some were plugged into nightlife, others knew where to find herbal remedies, and some shared their discounts to benefit the group as a whole. Despite the fluidity, we were a tight-knit community, bonded by our shared passion for skating and our willingness to support each other both on and off the rink.

One of my skate family members from that time, Sidney Davis, known as Cowboy, was skillfully captured by Robert Dea in recent years at Central Park, executing the same move. Often donning his signature leather cowboy hat and sometimes chaps, we cheer him on despite the memories of my own injury.

After High Roller closed, I frequented various rinks in Manhattan like Metropolis and Village Skating before finding my group of skate pals at Roxy on 18th Street and 10th Avenue. My passion for skating was solidified on that expansive maple floor, spoiled by the Robert Johnson-designed sound system and lighting.

I was fortunate to have great skate teachers within the Village Wizards, a part of the youth skating group Solar Rollers. We would meet early before the all-ages session, learning proper stretching techniques from members of the Alvin Ailey Dance Troupe. Marion Green's voice booming reminders of technique, such as "Why are you looking at the floor? Is it moving?" still resonate with me today, as I pass on those same words to new skaters decades later.

In those days, cameras were not as ubiquitous as they are now, making pictures from that era hard to come by. It was during the last showcase of the Solar Rollers that I stumbled upon the earliest picture of myself on skates, albeit without showing faces, taken by Angel Vargas, possibly the skate guard from my thunderstruck first visit to High Roller.

Our early morning skating groups seamlessly merged into the all-ages sessions that followed. Often, we would grab "dinner" at Blimpie before returning for the evening's adult session, marking the beginning of our rink rat days, where we spent over 15 hours on roller skates.

Becoming a rink rat and desiring employment marked a significant shift in my journey as a skater when I joined the team at Roxy, known as the Studio 54 of roller skating. Unlike the typical family fun center associated with rinks, Roxy held iconic status in the history of roller skating and rhythm skating culture in NYC. Landing a job there was a dream come true for a high school-aged kid.

In NYC, Empire in Brooklyn, alongside Good Skates and now Central Park Skate Circle, holds similar iconic status due to their vast exposure to skating from past to present. Unlike traditional rinks, Central Park Skate Circle is an outdoor venue. Personally, I align my skating style with the Bill Butler Jamma school. Rhythm skating, reliant on the beat of music—often R&B, Disco, and Dance Pop—best describes the type of skating I enjoy. Essentially, it's dancing on roller skates, expressing oneself in sync with the music, often in routines, couples skating, or group formations like trains and trios.

Transitioning to being part of the Roxy team separated me from other skaters. Suddenly, I was responsible for ensuring the well-being of fellow skaters, including the style's founder and other remarkable skaters of the time. It brought a burden—a heightened situational awareness, encompassing crowd safety, fire exits, multitasking conversations while scanning the floor, and recognizing potential security risks.

This heightened awareness also emphasized the critical role of the DJ in shaping the skate experience. While I was a capable skater, my focus was on maintaining safety and enjoyment for all, whether patrolling the floor or working the snack bar. Saturday nights in the mid-eighties at Roxy were bustling with over 1,000 skaters, grooving to skilled DJs like Robert Big Bob Clayton and DJ Juio. Working those nights earned me both money and experience.

Skating alongside the fastest skaters like David Cumming, known as Big Bird, was exhilarating yet challenging. Roxy's center rink, dubbed the "showoff circle," was a spectacle of skilled skaters, including the legendary Bill Butler and his partner "Little Mikey" Johnson, practicing amongst newcomers, affectionately called brownies. Witnessing synchronized routines and incredible moves by skaters like Scott "SloMo" Randolph was awe-inspiring—a testament to the talent and camaraderie within the skating community.

The compartmentalized conversations within our skate family led to some surprising encounters over the years when our different worlds collided. One morning, as I dragged myself to school after working a late skate session until 2:00 a.m., I stopped to chat with one of the school's security guards on the steps. The setting itself spoke volumes to those in the know—Bronx High School of Science's main entrance wasn't typically used except for dismissal or to get a late pass. Despite smoking being prohibited on campus and me being underage, the security guard didn't intervene as we talked about the Yankees.

As I conversed with the guard, I noticed a familiar gait approaching. As the person drew nearer, their teacher-like attire threw me off. But as they got closer, I realized it was my skate 'brother,' David Cancel, whom

I greeted with a big hug. Upon entering the school, I introduced him to the guard and learned that he was there to substitute as a health teacher. It made sense, considering his background in gymnastics alongside skating. Friends in his class reported that he was a good instructor, fair and effective. It felt awkward having skated with my brother until the early hours of the morning, only to see him at work a few hours later.

While I was undoubtedly intelligent, I wasn't a stellar student. My best subject was gym, where I enjoyed weightlifting and playing handball. School was an hour-long subway trip and walk from home, and with skate sessions on school nights running until 2:00 a.m., I became adept at napping. Skating and the associated nightlife took precedence over high school, making me one of the popular, cool kids. Although I managed academically, there were instances like forgetting about the SATs being held on a Saturday morning after working until 6:00 a.m. the night before. A cafe con leche y pancito fueled me after a brief nap, allowing me to achieve a 1280 on the SAT, a respectable score in general but considered just average among my classmates.

Working at Roxy also afforded me a ringside seat to witness the birth of hip hop as a commercially viable form of music. By the mid-eighties, interest in skating was waning, especially among the celebrity and fashion-conscious crowd that frequented NYC nightlife. To inject some glitz back into the club, the management turned to a promoter from the UK who introduced non-skating hip hop nights on Fridays.

One particularly hot Friday night brought about my most star-studded encounter. The club was packed early on, with the air conditioner struggling to keep up with the body heat. I ventured down the ramp in search of a cool breeze, hoping it wasn't tainted by the odors of the city. As fate would have it, the doorman at the ropes left momentarily, and I found myself in his place as a taxi pulled up.

As the doors opened, a figure rushed towards the ropes. Knowing most people couldn't jump a rope held at my head level, I instinctively reached out, only to find myself face to face with Steve Rubell, the former owner of Studio 54, accompanied by none other than Andy Warhol. Behind them stood Mick Jagger of the Rolling Stones. It was a surreal moment, nearly causing me to inadvertently block Jagger's path.

Later that night, another encounter occurred. While heading to the restroom in the VIP area, I was bumped by a man carrying beer bottles, causing the contents to spill on my skater shorts. Ready to react, I realized it was Mick Jagger again. My anger turned to embarrassment as I offered to replace the spilled beers, to which he kindly responded, "Sorry, mate."

Celebrities flocked to Roxy to witness DJs from the Bronx scratching records, creating new sounds that reflected the city's chaos. B-boys and breakdancers moved to these funky beats, adding to the club's vibrant atmosphere. I had the privilege of witnessing early performances by Madonna, Run DMC, The Beastie Boys, and many more hip hop pioneers.

Despite my focus on skating and dance music, my nights off often took me to a variety of musical events across the city. From punk and new wave bands at CBGBs to concerts by Chuck Berry and James Brown, my musical interests were eclectic. I also ventured with my skate family to other rinks in the city, where hip hop performances were incorporated into the skate sessions.

Ironically, as hip hop culture gained mainstream recognition, it became evident that the torch of dance skating was passing to hip hop. Graffiti art, introduced by hip hop, signaled a shift in the cultural landscape, indicating that it was time for dance skating to embrace this new era.

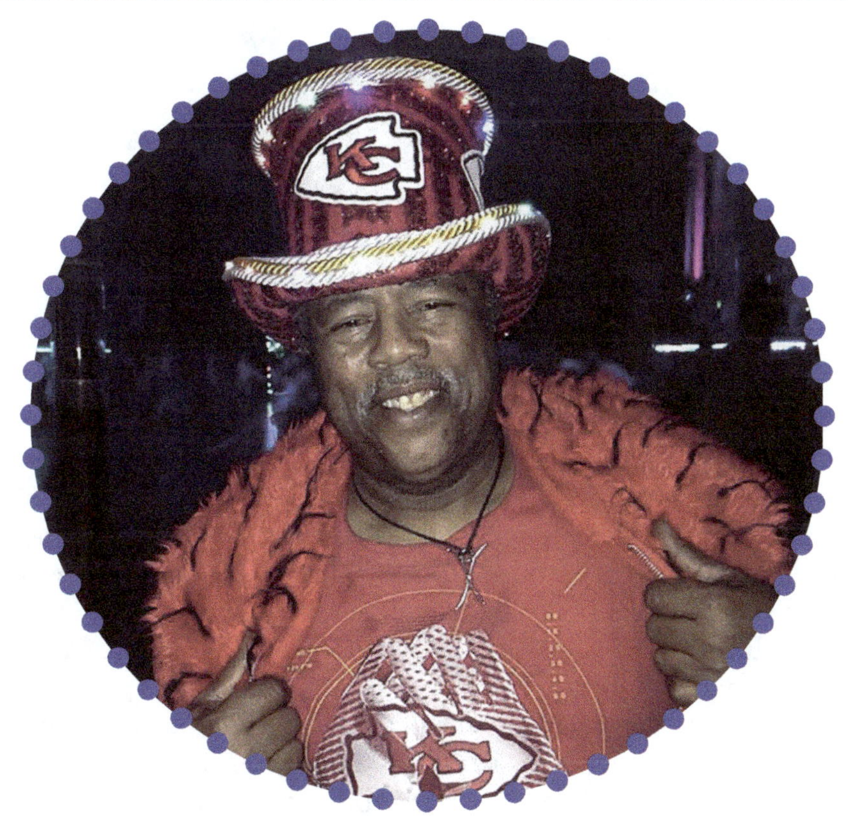

David Miles

aka The Godfather of Skate

Facebook: @David Miles | Instagram: @sfskater

"Spreading Rolligion"

The accolades bestowed upon me by the people of San Francisco include titles such as "The Godfather of Skating," "The Pied Piper of Skating," and "The Mayor of Golden Gate Park." For over four decades, I have been a passionate advocate for roller skating in all its forms, from dance and speed to slalom and marathon races. I've organized numerous skate-a-thons, including events like the Skate Against Hate, the Skate Against Violence, and the Skate Against Hunger, among others.

My dedication to spreading the joy of roller skating extends beyond San Francisco. I've donated skates to skaters in Kenya, and I've built mobile roller rinks for large events like Burning Man and the Electric Daisy Carnival. My mission, which I fondly call "Spreading Rolligion," aims to make roller skating accessible and enjoyable for people around the world.

Throughout my journey, I've had the opportunity to skate with mayors, negotiate with future governors, and even receive recognition from a president. I've been involved in ballot initiatives and legislation to make roller skating legal in San Francisco and throughout California. Each endeavor stems from my deep passion and devotion to roller skating.

Some of my skate events have gained global recognition. The San Francisco Friday Night Skate, for instance, has attracted thousands of inline skaters not only in the US but also in cities like London, Paris, Amsterdam, and South Africa. Additionally, I've cultivated a vibrant skate community at 6th Ave. Skatin' Place in Golden Gate Park and established my own roller rink, the Church of 8 Wheels, housed in a 140-year-old Catholic Church.

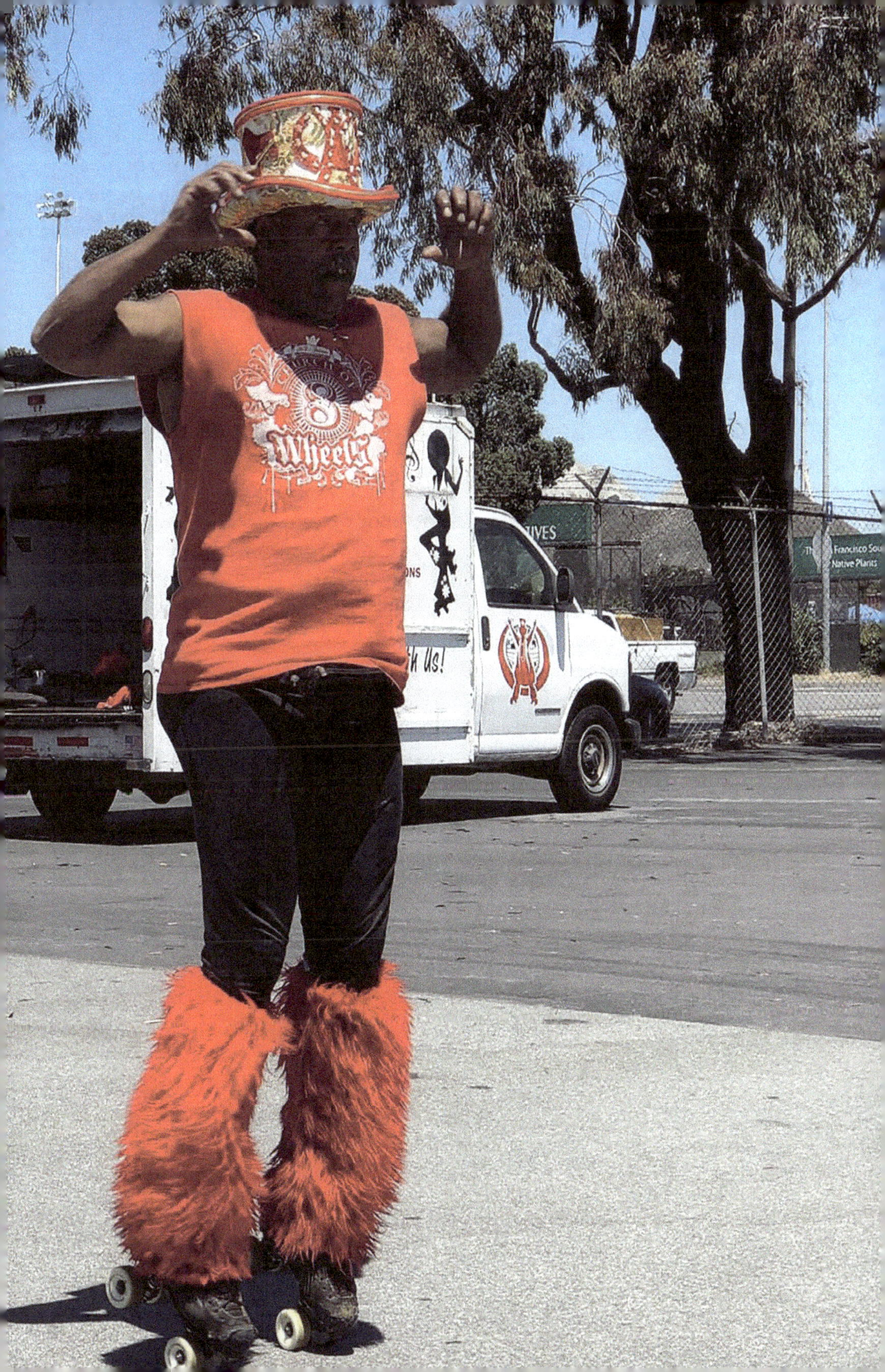
Wheels
Francisco
Native Plants

When it comes to my skate style, I don't conform to any particular style. I skate to the rhythm of the music, doing what feels right in the moment. Whether it's line dancing or performing my signature moves like the "Hat Spin" or quarter/half rubber leg moves, I let the beat guide me, especially when there's a funky groove.

My roller skating journey began in 1979 when I stumbled upon the vibrant skating scene in Golden Gate Park. Witnessing thousands of skaters gliding through the park on Sundays ignited a spark within me. Soon, I found myself skating almost every day, meeting fellow enthusiasts, and forming a community centered around our shared love for roller skating.

However, our skating paradise in Golden Gate Park faced threats of being shut down due to concerns about overcrowding and safety. In response, I joined the Roller Patrol, a group of volunteers tasked with ensuring safety and orderliness in the park. Through our efforts, roller skating was preserved in Golden Gate Park, and the success of the Skate Patrol paved the way for roller skating to thrive in the city.

As my involvement in roller skating grew, I organized events and fundraisers to promote the sport further. From the California Outdoor Roller-Skating Championships to the California Championship Series, I sought to showcase roller skating's diversity and athleticism. Despite challenges, such as the rise of inline skating, I continued to push boundaries and expand the reach of roller skating.

In the 1990s, I ventured into new territories, organizing events like the Napa Valley road skating race and partnering with Red Bull to produce the Great Skate freestyle championship series. I also played a pivotal role in establishing the Black Rock Roller Disco at Burning Man, transforming it into one of the event's most popular attractions.

Today, I am proud to be among the few African Americans who own a roller rink in the United States. The Church of 8 Wheels serves as a testament to my lifelong dedication to roller skating and my commitment to spreading joy and positivity through this beloved sport. Reflecting on my journey, I am grateful for the unwavering support of my family, especially my wife, whose faith in me has been a driving force behind my success. As Confucius once said, "Choose a job you love, and you'll never have to work a day in your life." And for me, roller skating is not just a job—it's a passion, a lifestyle, and a source of endless joy.

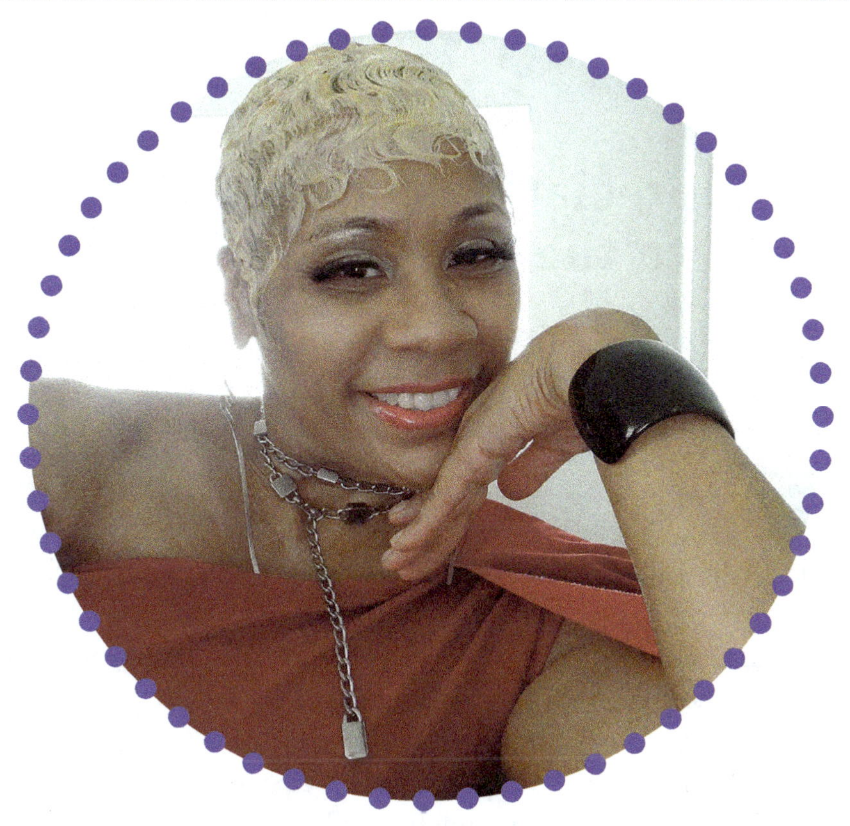

Sandice Jackson

Facebook: @Sandice Jackson

"Appreciate, Love, and Grow With the Culture, for it is an Evolution!"

Sandice Jackson, is the brainchild behind Breast Cancer Advocacy (BCA) & Shugar Infused (SI). She knows her educational foundation is just as important as her business expertise. Jackson's vision stretches far beyond the average eye; her vision includes helping others enhance their quality of life by improving their personal health, which is done by applying a positive attitude toward responsible, healthy life goals in a natural way.

With the motto, "Knowledge is Power" & "Courageous Courage," Jackson began building the foundation of her successful business over ten years ago. She intends to touch the hearts and minds of people from all walks of life so they can be equipped with the proper knowledge and education when they come to terms with the many challenges faced in the world to come, as it relates to living a natural healthy lifestyle. She intends to utilize her skills and expertise in herbal infusion, mentoring, motivating, training, educating, entertainment, and inspiring others.

Also know in the entertainment world for over ten years as Sandice Entertainment, Inc., Jackson has a love for motorcycle riding, stepping, and roller skating. She has introduced some form of creative entertainment service in all these areas. She has a love for artistic style skating because it allows her to use her creativity on wheels while giving her a sense of freedom and mental release that's soothing to the soul.

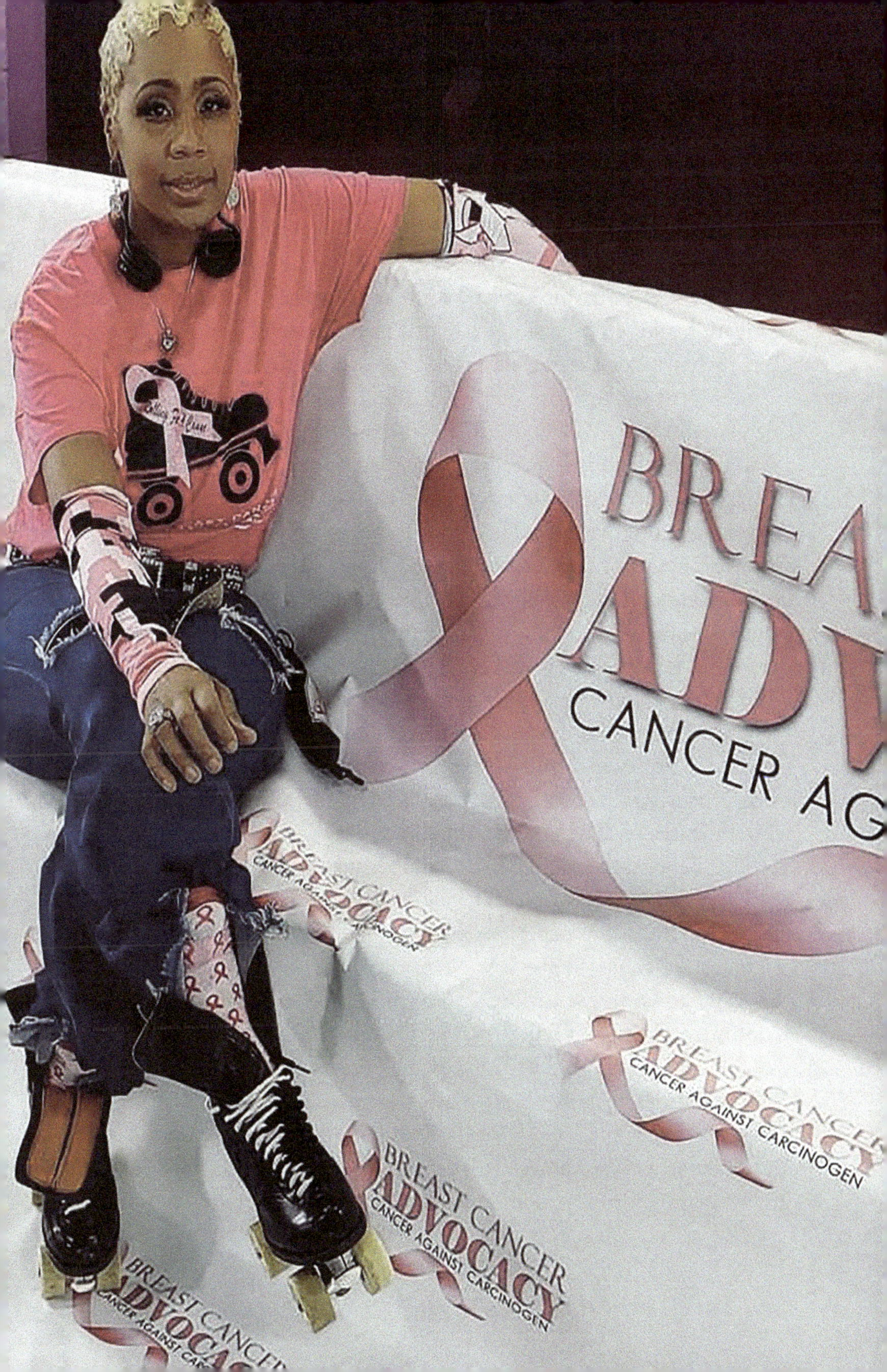
BREAST CANCER
ADVOCACY
CANCER AGAINST CARCINOGEN
BREAST CANCER
ADVOCACY
CANCER AGAINST CARCINOGEN

She started skating when she was a young girl with her older brothers at Skate City, The Loop, and once she got older, Glenwood Roller Rink. She then went on to pursue other important life ventures, which required her to put the love for roller skating on hold. Sometime later in life, she was inspired by a great legendary skater with great motivation and teaching skills to revisit the wonderful wood of skating. Quickly her roller-skating skills then came back to life!

She went on to skate at places like The Rink, Rich City Skate, Glenwood, Fleet Wood, Markham Skating Rink, and many rinks on a national level, and have been skating ever since. Her love for roller skating and stepping (which goes hand in hand) also inspired her to do skate jams along with all-white yacht parties under her organization Sandice Entertainment, Inc., so that others could share in her creativity of the skate and stepping culture. She presented special skaters and steppers with trophies, plates, and other special awards to recognize, inspire, and give back to the love and culture of skating and stepping.

Jackson, a known business guru, serves as President of Operations for both organizations. Jackson's previous corporate and personal experience prepared her as an executive in the field of natural healthy living, focusing on cancer against carcinogens and herbal infusion, which focuses on having a healthy mind, body, and emotions.

She believes changing lives could cause a life-changing chain reaction in the way people eat, talk, act, and feel about their worth, health, wealth, and prosperity.

Sandice would like everyone from one end of the universe to the other to continue to love and appreciate the cultures of skating. Continue to help your fellow skaters to appreciate, love, and grow with the culture, for it is an EVOLUTION!

You can learn more about Sandice and what she continues to do across all social media platforms; look for Sandice Jackson, Shugar Infused, and Breast Cancer Advocacy. You can also visit her websites at: www.shugarinfused.com and www.mybreastcanceradvocacy.org.

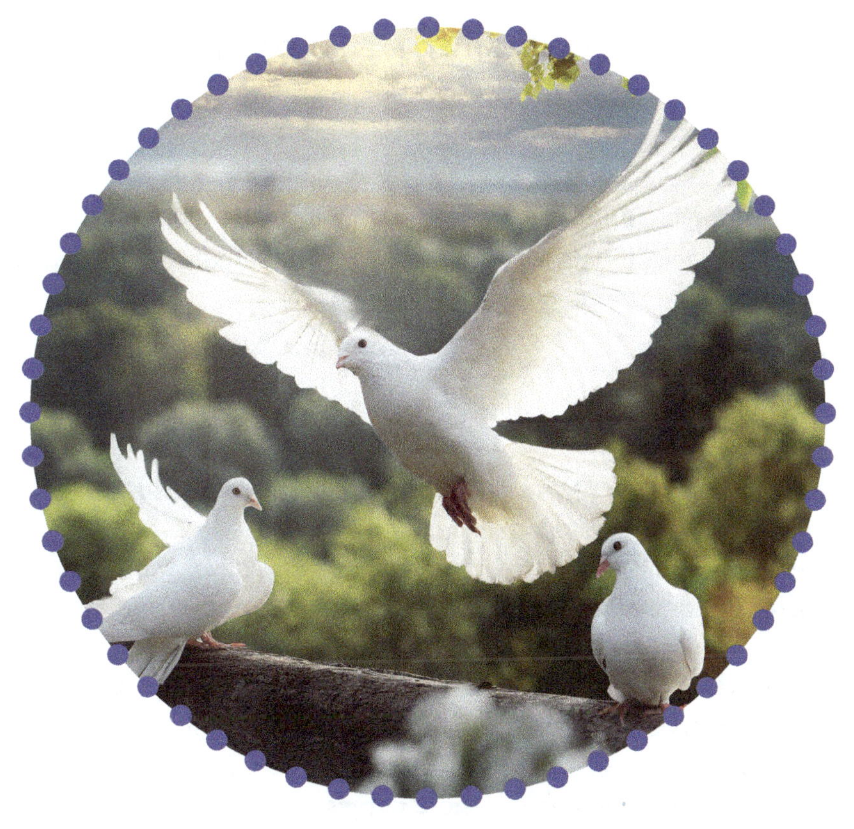

In Memoriam

"Gone But Not Forgotten"

"What we once enjoyed and deeply loved we can never lose, for all that we love deeply becomes a part of us."
— Helen Keller (1880-1968)

We wish to take this opportunity to honor Theresa "Ms. Tee" Jones for her love and passion for the art. A soul taken too soon. Our tribute begins with her son and extends to her skate family:

Mommy, Mom, Mother, Grandma, Grandmother, Confidant, Healer, Comforter Nurse, Prayer Warrior, Friend but I always called you Mom.

You lived up to each one of these names and then some. I can never put 53 years of life into words to describe all that you meant to me and your Granddaughter's. We love and miss you so much, oh how selfishly we wish you could still be here, but we understand God was ready for you to rest.

You lived a full life here on earth and now you are enjoying eternal life in Heaven.

Skate and Dance on Momma...... ~ Reginald Mills

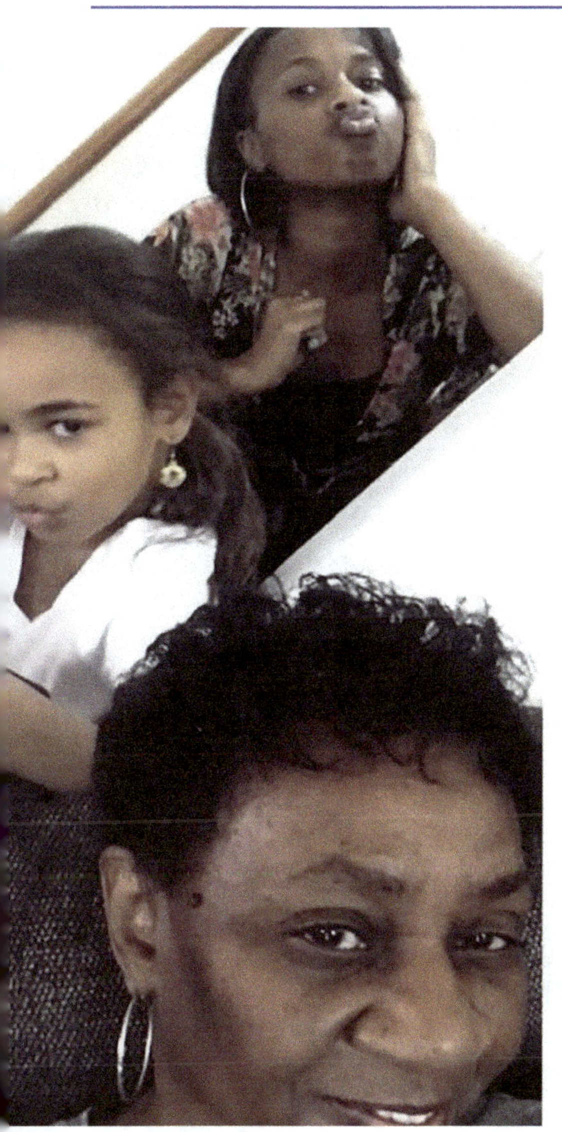

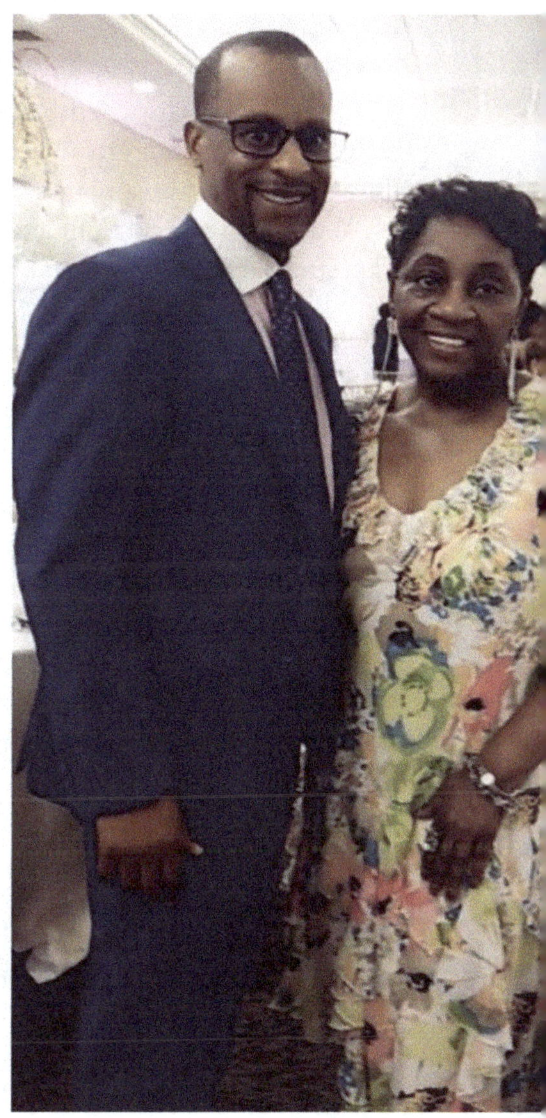

Tee was like a mother, sister, great side kick partner. My skating travel partner, workout motivator, ball room dance partner, all around supporter and person you could go to and talk to. ~Antonio Vant

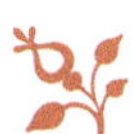

Mom Tee

"One of my many mentors, teacher, and ultimate ladies of ladies. This photo was taken at the first Houston round up where you were riding a horse and hurt your shoulder and said, "that horse won't stop me". You fought a good fight and god is the "best" knower... forever love and eternal "respect" mom rest in power!!!!!" ~Ice from Philly

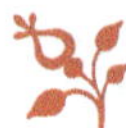

Goodbyes are not forever. Goodbyes are not the end. They simply mean I will miss you until we meet again. Ms. Tee RIP and you always be with us. ~ Myesha McCaskill aka Smooth Goddess

When I needed advice on life and a pound cake, Theresa "Tee" aka "Betty Crocker" was the person who helped me navigate through it, she will NEVER BE FORGOTTEN. ~ Richard Houston aka Rocking Richard

Ms. Tee was very respectful, she was always smiling and saying hello, so friendly. God will always be with you, keep on smiling all the way up in heaven. All your travels on this earth are over and you will be missed. Sending blessings to her and her family may she rest in peace and keep on rolling in Heaven. The Washington family love's you and we will miss you on the wood.

~ Peace and Love Henry Washington and family

Ms. Theresa Jones "Miss Tee" was so well known in Detroit that no one needed to speak her last name. In fact, in the rink all you had to say was "Tee" and everyone knew who you were talking about. I witnessed her providing counsel and guidance to young, mid-age and old. She was kind, friendly, motherly and a gift to all who came to know her. Tee was equally known in the dance community and to see her dancing was a treat. Non-skaters knew Tee because of her cooking and baking skills. To be absent from the body is to be present with the Lord. May she rest in eternal peace. We miss you Tee! ~ Kevin H. Williams

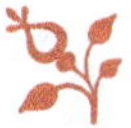

Her smile could outshine the sun.

Her wise words always enlightened and encouraged me. Her moves on the skate floor were soulful and fun to watch. Her dance moves off the skate floor were delightful to see. Her beautiful spirit left in our hearts will remain forever.

Ms. Tee, you are sorely missed.

Until we meet again Queen ~ Khannie Butler

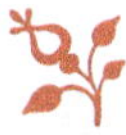

We all will miss you Tee. My most memorable time spent with you was on this cruise (my first cruise) with The Royal Caribbean Cruise line. The Detroit Rhythmic Rollers did a wonderful job putting this trip together and we even got to Skate on the ship. You fought the Good Fight, now rest my Sister. ~ Love always, Joi Loftin

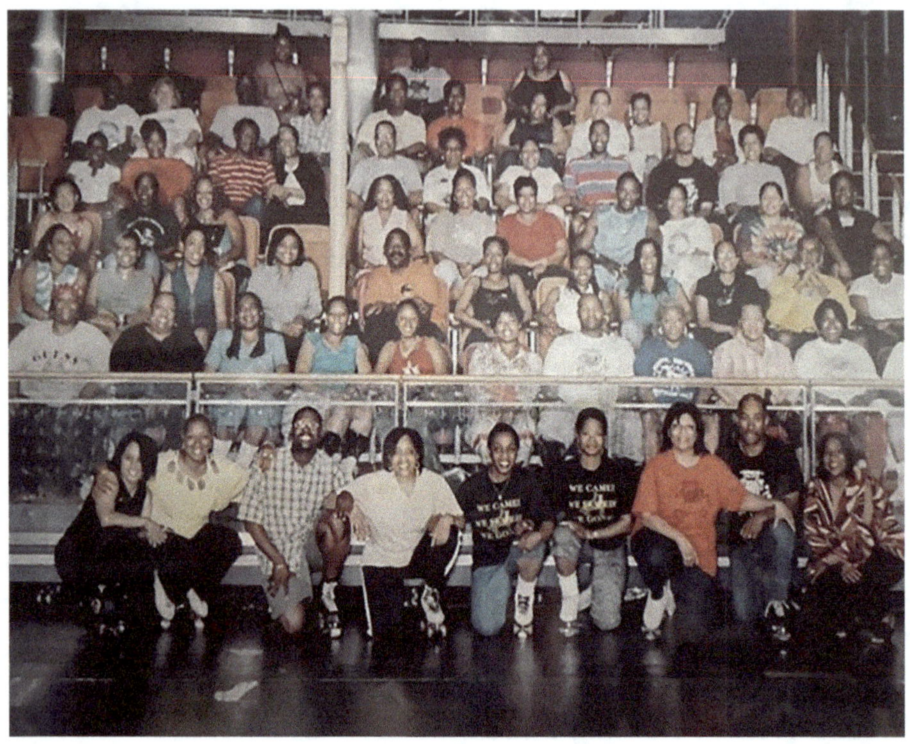

Sending peace and prayers to those in the skate world whom we have lost but whom shall never be forgotten:

Honey Boy
Bill White
Nacear Gredic
Darren "Dj Knoc"
Kolibaba

For those not mentioned, you will forever be in our hearts, prayers and in our souls with each roll of our wheels.

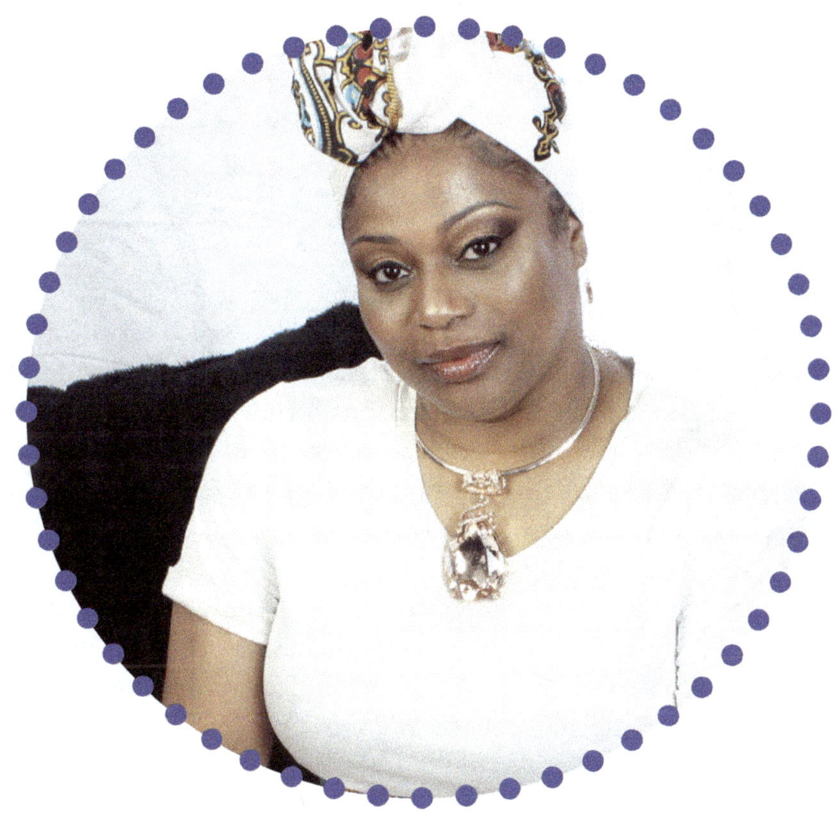

Amirah Palmer

Facebook: @Amirah Palmer | Instagram: @itsamirahpalmer

"About the Lead Author"

Amirah Palmer is not just a skater; she is a visionary, serial entrepreneur, and the founder and CEO of Sk8rz Konnect. Her platform, Sk8rz Konnect, serves as a showcase for the diverse skills and artistry found in various forms of skating, including roller, ice, and skateboarding. Amirah is a decorated U.S. Army Veteran, an International Best Selling Author, and a graduate of the University of Maryland. Her passion extends to volunteering and community service.

Through The Evolution of Skating series, Amirah Palmer aims to create a unified platform that brings together every genre of the skating arts. Her goal is to connect, showcase, and inspire skaters in their respective fields, fostering a sense of community and encouragement within the skating world.

www.ingramcontent.com/pod-product-compliance
Lightning Source LLC
LaVergne TN
LVHW050536100826
845148LV00002B/584

* 9 7 9 8 9 8 6 5 2 7 2 9 1 *